"Fuller's 2023 Missiology Lectures drew a record number of eight hundred people to this hybrid event to hear the stellar line-up of presenters on the topic of evangelism. Their contributions, now brought together in this volume, rescue the practice from distortions, reconnect it with the broader Christian mission, and re-vision the evangel for post-Christendom. *Evangelism Next* will critically engage a diverse world in ways that are inviting, transformative, foster liberation and justice, and aim at reconciliation."

—KIRSTEEN KIM
Paul E. Pierson Professor of World Christianity, Fuller Theological Seminary

"This book aims to challenge head-on the conflation of evangelism and various forms of colonialism. Without abandoning the former but eschewing the latter, this volume exhibits creative models that offer compelling evangelistic alternatives without the baggage that the next generation might find objectionable. This is truly a holistic, twenty-first-century mission which is both fresh and biblically oriented, shedding the unnecessary accretions which have proven to be deterrents to the spread of God's kingdom in this world."

—ALLEN YEH,
Dean, International Theological Seminary

"This volume is a state-of-the-art smorgasbord—a collection that challenges the cultural captivity of evangelism and introduces fresh, holistic, and Spirit-driven possibilities for sharing the evangel. I recommend it to all readers concerned about the cooptation of Christian witness by whiteness and empire."

—COLLIN CORNELL
Assistant Professor of Bible and Mission, Fuller Theological Seminary

Evangelism Next

Evangelism Next

De-Constructing and Re-Constructing Evangelism

Edited by

Soong-Chan Rah,

Julie B. Scott,

& Sean M. Watkins

PICKWICK *Publications* • Eugene, Oregon

EVANGELISM NEXT
De-Constructing and Re-Constructing Evangelism

Cascade Books
An Imprint of Wipf and Stock Publishers
199 W. 8th Ave., Suite 3
Eugene, OR 97401

www.wipfandstock.com

PAPERBACK ISBN: 979-8-3852-2991-8
HARDCOVER ISBN: 979-8-3852-2992-5
EBOOK ISBN: 979-8-3852-2993-2

Cataloguing-in-Publication data:

Names: Rah, Soong-Chan, editor. | Scott, Julie B., editor. | Watkins, Sean M., editor.

Title: Evangelism next : de-constructing and re-constructing evangelism / edited by Soong-Chan Rah, Julie B. Scott, and Sean M. Watkins.

Description: Eugene, OR : Cascade Books, 2026 | Includes bibliographical references.

Identifiers: ISBN 979-8-3852-2991-8 (paperback) | ISBN 979-8-3852-2992-5 (hardcover) | ISBN 979-8-3852-2993-2 (ebook)

Subjects: LCSH: Evangelicalism—History—21st century. | Church history—21st century. | Evangelistic work. | Church renewal. | Evangelistic work—History. | Witness bearing (Christianity). | Missions.

Classification: BV3790 .E935 2026 (paperback) | BV3790 (ebook)

VERSION NUMBER 05/27/26

Contents

Introduction

Soong-Chan Rah

In recent years, evangelism as a church practice has come under scrutiny. Certain Western-centric, patriarchal, racially and culturally insensitive expressions of evangelism have been mistaken as the norm in church life and are now being eschewed as no longer practical or applicable in twenty-first-century Christianity. While the practice of evangelism has been challenged, the need for communicating the *evangel* has increased, particularly in the US context. Many are leaving the church while still claiming faith in Jesus. Others are abandoning their faith altogether. Others are questioning aspects of evangelism and Christian faith. Still others have little to no connection or experience with the Christian gospel message.

Expressions of disconnecting with the Christian religion in the United States have been popularly labeled as "deconstruction." Seen as hostile and potentially destructive to the church, the work of "deconstruction" may actually serve as a necessary expression of evangelism in a post-Christendom era. "Deconstruction" must be more clearly identified and expressed as a theological and ecclesial process, a necessary prelude to move towards acts of "reconstruction" or "re-formation" that could signal a more biblical, relevant, and applicable expression of evangelism in the contemporary context.

A question that drives the conversations throughout this text: "Is Evangelism passe—a remnant of a previous generation's efforts to spread its particular iteration and expression of Christianity?" The "Four Spiritual Laws" and its assertion of immutability may invoke resistance from a different generation of believers. Confrontational apologetics in its US iteration may justify a format of engagement that is actually more political than biblical. The cultural and generational particularity of evangelism may even result in the rejection of the basic idea of evangelism by the next generation of Christians. These challenges require the church to do the hard work of self-examination to discern what evangelism could look like. For some, addressing these challenges has been defined as deconstructionism. But the challenge offered in this text is not simply to deconstruct but to reconstruct evangelism. To effectively address these challenges, we need to better understand these terms, often used haphazardly and needing deeper academic reflection and insight.

The contemporary expression of evangelism in the United States is deeply shaped by its entanglement with Western cultural assumptions. In the field of evangelism, Western cultural captivity has had multiple expressions. In *The Next Evangelicalism: Freeing the Church from Western Cultural Captivity*, I identify three characteristics of Western culture that dominate Evangelical Christianity. The hyper-individualism of Western culture prioritizes personal faith and salvation, which stands in stark contrast to the communal expression of faith found in the Scriptures. The consumerism and materialism of Western society find expression in evangelistic efforts as methods of evangelism are mass-produced, often distorting the gospel as a commodity for personal gain. Racism and cultural chauvinism also center the Western perspective in evangelism, excluding and marginalizing non-white voices. An additional analysis of Western evangelism should include the patriarchal systems that have silenced the voices of women in the communication of the gospel. The deconstruction of these dysfunctional narratives is a necessary part of reforming the existing practice of evangelism.

The power of these narratives and the imagination supporting them requires a deconstruction of the narratives in order to reconstruct and develop new narratives. If the dominant narratives of evangelism have justified colonialism, slavery, and genocide, then the extant dysfunction must be challenged so that new narratives may emerge. Simply asserting, repeating, or refraining from the existing narratives will not change embedded practices. Instead, the church must embrace counternarratives—stories that disrupt the status quo, amplify marginalized voices, and reimagine the community of faith as a reconciled and justice-seeking community. This process of de-construction is not about destroying church practices, but about freeing it from the limitations of cultural captivity so that it might bear faithful, transformative witness to the gospel in a changing world.

This text brings together leading voices and fresh perspectives to examine how evangelism must be re-formed for the twenty-first century. Emerging from the Missiology Lectures at Fuller Theological Seminary in the fall of 2023, this text offers a collection of presentation from those proceedings. Moving beyond inherited paradigms, deconstructing dysfunctional narratives, and reconstructing practices that are faithful to the core message of the gospel, this text invites readers to reflect critically on both the challenges and the promises of sharing the good news in our complex world.

In Part I (drawn from the plenary sessions of the 2023 Fuller Missiology Lectures), the text offers aspects of de-construction that may be helpful in the movement towards a new evangelism. Chapter 1, "(Re)forming Evangelism," lays the groundwork for this conversation. David Zac Niringiye and Soong-Chan Rah chart the necessity of balancing deconstruction with reconstruction, urging the church to shed the cultural captivity of Western Evangelicalism and embrace a contextual, narrative-driven faith. In chapter 2, "God-Gifted Interruptions," Ruth Padilla DeBorst reflects on the unpredictable movement of God's Spirit through a sermon offered at the 2023 Missiology Lectures. Drawing from her Latin American experience and the story of Paul and Silas in Philippi, she challenges the obsession with strategies and measurable outcomes that marks much of contemporary evangelism. In chapter 3, "Global Evangelism," Vinoth Ramachandra explores the complexity of Christian mission in an interconnected and pluralistic world. He advocates for an incarnational, dialogical approach, one that listens deeply, engages courageously, and seeks unity amid profound diversity. In chapter 4, "Tom Skinner and Black Power Evangelicalism," Jemar Tisby explores Tom Skinner's role in intersecting Black Power ideals with Evangelical Christianity. Skinner's life and ministry offered a deconstruction of the existing narratives of evangelism. In chapter 5, "Dangerous Women and the Promise of Purity," Jessica Wai-Fong Wong interrogates the history and theology behind purity culture and the regulation of women's bodies within Christian tradition. She calls the church to a new imagination, moving us beyond the dysfunctional imagination of patriarchy.

Part II (which draws from a selection of the breakout sessions that were conducted at the 2023 Fuller Missiology Lectures) shifts the focus to different models and examples of the re-construction of evangelism leading to the reformation of evangelism through a more holistic and global lens. Part II offers a more practitioner and constructive applied theology approach to the topic of evangelism. Drawing from the work of INFEMIT, the International Fellowship for Mission as Transformation, chapter 6 by Al Tizon and Ruth Padilla DeBorst, examines the topic "Mission as Transformation," a holistic, global approach to evangelism. In chapter 7, "Evangelism Among People of Other Faiths," Jose Abraham, Darren Duerksen, and Vinod John bring fresh insight into evangelism across religions. Chapter 8, "Evangelism on Fire," is a collaborative chapter compiled by Pentecost Theological Seminary in Ghana. The authors—David Nyansah Hayfron, Amos Jimmy Markin, Rebecca Sey, Christian Tsekpoe, and Okyere Walker—offer a grassroots, Spirit-empowered approach to evangelism that emerges from practices among Pentecostal churches in Ghana. Chapter 9, "Communal Evangelism from the Margins," is coauthored by Alexia Salvatierra and Brandon Wrencher. Drawing from their seminal text, *Buried Seeds: Learning from the Vibrant Resilience of Marginalized Christian Communities*, the chapter examines how marginalized Christian communities have embodied communal evangelism and holistic discipleship. In chapter 10, Len Tang offers an expression of evangelism that has been re-constructed as he offers "Church Plants as Evangelism Laboratories." Chapter 11, "The Incarcerated Church," coauthored by Jarrett Keith and Soong-Chan Rah, narrates the possibility of learning from the marginalized community of the incarcerated. Included in the chapter are the voices of several incarcerated individuals who have practiced evangelism through the incarcerated church.

Together, these chapters offer a road map for reimagining evangelism—one that is rooted in critical reflection, humility, and hope. They invite readers to move beyond inherited models and toward practices that are contextually aware, justice-oriented, and open to the surprising work of the Spirit. As Christianity's global landscape continues to change, so too must our understanding of what it means to bear faithful witness to the good news today.

PART I

De-Constructing Evangelism

Chapter 1

Re-Forming Evangelism

David Zac Niringiye and Soong-Chan Rah

In this chapter, two authors, situated in two different continents and multiple contexts of ministry and evangelism offer the importance of balancing the work of de-construction with the work of re-construction. Deconstructing evangelism necessitates a movement away from the Western cultural captivity of the church and offers a necessary corrective to dysfunctional expressions of evangelism. Reconstructing evangelism allows a forward movement that can result in a reformation of evangelism. In this chapter, we attempt to define these terms in a way that projects us towards the next iteration of evangelism.

Deconstruction vs. De-Construction

"Deconstruction" is the current, in-vogue term used for any conversation critiquing the current state of Christianity. The term has been linked more broadly to postmodern philosophy and applied more specifically to Gen Y and Gen Z leaving the faith in large numbers and labeled as "de-churched." Deconstruction has been associated with postmodern philosophy, which is often relegated as an extreme, anti-Christian, and secular worldview. Deconstruction, therefore, has a strong, negative connotation as a form of modern apostasy.

However, deconstruction, as currently applied in the Christian context, is not the specific, technical term of deconstruction associated with postmodern philosophy. The specific, postmodern expression of deconstruction emerges from semiotics, the study of signs. Postmodern philosopher Jacques Derrida (whose academic discipline is semiotics and linguistics) offers seminal reflections on the postmodern project of deconstruction. Derrida states, "The absence of a transcendental sign extends the domain and the play of significations infinitely."[1] Using technical language specific to the discipline of semiotics, Derrida explains how a sign (words and symbols) signifies a specific meaning, based upon a system of language that assigns a signification (meaning) to the sign. Deconstruction removes or devalues the system of language, thereby removing the limits to a definition of a specific word. In other words, words can mean whatever we determine them to be, not what an external language system determines them to be.

Derrida's academic definition reveals the specificity of the term "deconstruction" and its particular usage in semiotics and postmodern philosophy. Stanley Grenz summarizes "deconstruction" by asserting, "Derrida thus holds that meaning is never static, never given once-for-all. Instead, meaning changes over time and with changing contexts. . . . For Derrida, there is no 'outside the text.' All we have is the text itself, not some external meaning to which the text points. The 'book' is actually our 'reading' of the text. . . . But this means that the text is fluid. It has no fixed origin, identity, or end."[2] Deconstruction, in its postmodern expression, removes authorial intent from the equation of meaning and interpretation and allows for the re-assignment of meaning, removing specific signification of texts.

The irony is that those who are fearful of deconstruction are actually engaging in the act of deconstruction. They are taking a word that means one thing in a specific context and using that word to make it mean whatever they want it to mean. It is akin to many Evangelicals who use "woke" and "CRT," not with their original intention and accurate definition but make them mean whatever they want them to mean, weaponizing them as slurs to denigrate their opponents. In the same way, "deconstruction" has been used to mean whatever suits a particular agenda and demeans those who are engaged in the act of challenging the presuppositions of the church.

The specific and maybe extreme usage of the term "deconstruction" in postmodern philosophy, therefore, does not align with what may be happening with Gen Y and Gen Z. There is great anxiety around the negative

1. Derrida, *Writing and Difference*, 280.

2. Grenz, *Primer on Postmodernism*, 144, 146.

influence of postmodern philosophy on these generations, but their acts of "deconstruction" do not emerge from an application of extreme postmodern principles rooted in semiotics. To associate the reflections and questions of younger generations (and others) with a catchphrase that has a specific meaning and usage is inaccurate and inappropriate.

The emerging (and current) generations are not deconstructing their faith; they are "*de*-constructing" their faith (note the hyphen). "De-constructing" faith challenges the extant systems and structures of Christianity that may be problematic in their current expressions. De-construction, therefore, is more reminiscent of a "re-forming" of Christian faith. De-construction may be the precursor for re-formation. They may be tearing down dysfunctional, Western Evangelical constructs that may be the actual obstruction to the work of evangelism, rather than simply questioning the meaning of specific, Evangelical assignments of meaning to specific practices and terms. De-construction, in its current expression among Evangelicals, therefore, may be a necessary practice that opens the door for contextual applications of Christian faith, which can positively re-form Christian faith in a relevant and applicable manner for the next generation of believers.

De-Construction and Re-Construction

The necessary de-construction of the current iteration and expression of evangelism should engage the dysfunctional narratives embedded in the current systems, particularly in the US expressions of evangelism. This confrontation is necessary because of the power of narratives to shape and reshape culture, society, the church, and the systems and structures of those institutions. In *Unsettling Truths*,[3] my coauthor, Mark Charles, and I examine the power of narratives through the paradigms of social reality offered by Peter Berger and Thomas Luckmann in their seminal work *The Social Construction of Reality*.[4] Narratives are the internalized stories and values that shape social reality. Because narratives are internalized, they are much more difficult to confront and overcome.

For example, while the system of chattel slavery and the individuals who perpetuated it were overcome through both individual and structural confrontations, the narrative of white supremacy persevered and was able

3. Charles and Rah, *Unsettling Truths*.

4. Berger and Luckmann, *Social Construction of Reality*.

to rebuild dysfunctional systems based upon a diseased narrative and imagination. While the system of chattel slavery no longer operates, the system of Jim Crow emerged in its place and was empowered by the existing fuel of white supremacy. In the same way, when the system of Jim Crow was torn down, the narrative fuel of white supremacy remained untouched and was able to build the system of the New Jim Crow in its place. Narratives become internalized within systems and proceed to replicate systems that allow the full expression of their dysfunctional narratives.

The necessary de-construction of the dysfunctional aspects of evangelism requires a confrontation of evil in its proper geography.[5] Dysfunctional, and even sinful, expressions of evangelism in the individual, evil expressions of evangelism in the system, and diseased expressions of evangelism in narratives all require a confrontation on the level of its dysfunction. The task of a proper de-construction that leads to re-formation of evangelism is to expose the extant, diseased imagination and narratives that have shaped the theologically dysfunctional imaginations and narratives.[6]

In *The Next Evangelicalism*, multiple aspects of US Evangelicalism are identified as captive more to Western culture than to the tenets of Scripture.[7] These expressions of a diseased, Western imagination have shaped US Evangelicalism and the evangelistic expressions of US Evangelicalism. I posit that hyper-individualism, excessive materialism, and consumerism, along with racism, cultural chauvinism, and toxic masculinity have negatively shaped the culture of US Evangelicalism. This cultural captivity reveals the dysfunctional imagination and narratives that have shaped US Evangelicalism and US expressions of evangelism. These dysfunctional systems, structures, narratives, and imagination require de-construction.

The proper de-construction, and the subsequent re-construction and re-formation of evangelism is an appropriate response to our current social reality, both within the church and in the world. The subsequent generations' desire and need to de-construct the previous generations' expression of evangelism (which may actually prove to be dysfunctional and irrelevant to the current iteration of Christianity) could be a positive step in the appropriate re-formation and reformation of our faith. Both terms become positive, constructive actions: re-formation (positively forming and shaping the faith) and reformation (an act of reform or positive change).

5. Mott, *Biblical Ethics and Social Change*.

6. See also Prior, *Evangelical Imagination*.

7. Rah, *Next Evangelicalism*.

Evangelism, as specifically expressed over the last fifty years in US Evangelicalism, has had a specific and useful application, because it spoke to a specific context. In a Western, modern worldview that emphasized reason and rationality, expressed in specific, Western philosophical assumptions, such as Scottish Common-Sense philosophy and linear and dialectical models of development, the modes and expressions of evangelism felt appropriate and relevant. The "Four Spiritual Laws"[8] and "Evidence that Demands a Verdict"[9] became entrenched as key evangelistic tools for the mid-twentieth century Evangelical movement and emerged from the linear and Western philosophical mindset of its time. These structures and forms had a specific connection to a particular context: the modern, Western worldview. The expression of evangelism was contextual but with an underlying structure. The contextual expression of reason and rationality served as an open door to the gospel, because it was specific to a cultural context. These specific expressions and constructs were built on a foundation of Scripture and theological reflection. De-construction examines the false constructs. In order to better understand these false constructs, context must be examined.

If the modern construct of reason and rationality drives our current evangelistic efforts, then the problematic elements of the modern construct can and should be called into question by subsequent iterations and expressions of Christianity. If the modern construct of rationality and reason resulted in the oppression of one race over the other because it seemed reasonable at the time, then the construct that led these "rational" assumptions needs de-construction. If the modern construct makes certain patriarchal assumptions, then de-construction is necessary for the gospel message to be impactful for the next generation. The work of the church is not a reassigning of meaning without context (deconstruction), but an attempt to better understand context (de-construction) to better form relevant and applicable expressions of evangelism (re-construction).

De-construction of the dysfunctional expressions of evangelism and the re-construction of evangelism, therefore, is part of the necessary reformation of the church. As social contexts change, the church adapts to the changes. When Western society moved from the centrality of European empire to more democratic and republican forms of governance, the church adapted accordingly. As Christianity moves from a Western-centric

8. Bright, *Four Spiritual Laws.*

9. McDowell and McDowell, *Evidence That Demands a Verdict.*

demographic to a much larger, global demographic, then the church needs to adapt accordingly. The practice of de-construction is a necessary part of redefining and re-forming the church. It was an act of re-formation that renewed the church through the Protestant Reformation, de-constructing the dysfunctional expressions of the dominant religious powers and offering new paradigms for the spread of the gospel. It was an act of re-formation that renewed the church through the growth of global Christianity and the subsequent new paradigms that continue to emerge from this reality.

New models of evangelism are not necessarily a categorical rejection of the old models, but rather, an acceptance of the new realities in which evangelism now operates. New models of evangelism must move beyond cultural captivity and build on the historical and theological foundations of the proclamation and demonstration of the gospel message. New models of evangelism must engage the current cultural reality as well as engage the future potential and direction of the church. The challenge for the church is how to share the gospel through a "truth-possessed" versus "truth-pursued" paradigm. The old models of evangelism focused on a "truth-possessed" approach. The church "owns" the truth, and therefore, the task of evangelism is simply downloading our version of truth upon the other. This approach, given the cultural context of modernity, resulted in severe dysfunction in the church. The "truth-pursued" approach acknowledges the frailty of human existence. It acknowledges that the church's task is not to *own* the truth but to *pursue* the truth. The pursuit of truth requires the humility of the church to de-construct, re-construct, and re-form the truth. Our task, therefore, is not simply to de-construct, but also to re-construct. Through this "both/and" action, we may be participating in the positive re-formation of our faith, which may be what is needed for the next evangelism.

De-Construction from a Global Perspective

Shifting from a US-based perspective to a broader, global perspective, the disaffection in the West with church and Christian faith, and the apparent disconnect with the Christian gospel, is an opportunity to interrogate not only dominant patterns and practices of evangelism but its content. It should force us to grapple afresh with the question "What is the *evangel*?" and the corollary "What are means and ways of communicating the *evangel* that are performances of the *evangel* itself?" Making the distinction between Christianity and the *evangel* is essential: Christianity is not the *evangel*; the *evangel* is not Christianity. The Greek word *evangel* brings us back to the essential meaning of "good news" rather than what has become the cultural trappings of the word "gospel" used in the US Evangelical context. The good news of Jesus' birth, life, death, resurrection, and ascension, as expressed, is the full meaning of *evangel*.

To deepen our conversation, we need to integrate epistemes beyond Western paradigms—those which are rooted in histories and geographies other than the West. Here, we are asking the question whether there is a rationale for de-construction from geographies and histories for whom postmodern is not the defining narrative—for coming to grips with the critical urgency for de-construction. In broadening the scope of our sources for defining de-construction, and by drawing from other language systems other than those shaped by modernity and postmodernity, we may be freed from the hyphenated distinction to which the English language consigns us.

Every culture and era grapples with how language functions in embodying and communicating meaning. Language is the quintessential embodiment of meaning-making systems and processes. The language systems of many cultures in sub-Saharan Africa are rooted in a primal worldview. "Primal," here, must be distinguished from the pejorative term "primitive"; "primal" refers to "the thought patterns, perceptions of reality, and the concept of identity and community" prior to the encounter with Western culture (embedded in education systems and religion).[10] Primal has two features: "their historical anteriority and their basic, elemental status in human experience."[11] For them, meaning is not consigned primarily to words, or for that matter, text (in the modern sense). The key to meaning and meaning making is story, because life and living is perceived as story or the interaction of stories. Each "person-being" is a story: an embodiment of many stories as well as a "person-becoming" in the process of encountering and making sense of new experiences.

Story and narrative should not be understood simply as the social and cultural activity of sharing stories for entertainment, or teaching some lesson, value, or life skills, but rather as an episteme. Who we are, how we self-identify, and how we make sense of our location in the world are the stories we have inherited and been told—and tell ourselves and the world. We are all narrators, because we embody stories, *particular* stories. Moreover, narration is itself part of the essence of personhood. H. Porter Abbott put it

10. Bediako, *Christianity in Africa*, 93.

11. Walls, *Missionary Movement*, 121.

well, that narrative is "something we all engage in, artists and non-artists alike. We make narratives many times a day, every day of our lives. And we start doing so almost from the moment we begin to put words together."[12]

Katongole states,

> Stories not only shape how we view reality but also how we respond to life and indeed the very sort of persons we become. In other words, we are how we imagine ourselves and how others imagine us. . . . Who we are, and who we are capable of becoming, depends very much on the stories we tell, the stories we listen to, and the stories we live. Stories not only shape our values, aims, and goals; they define the range of what is desirable and what is possible. Stories, therefore, are not simply fictional narratives meant for our entertainment; stories are part of our social ecology. They are embedded in us and form the very heart of our cultural, economic, religious, and political worlds. This applies not only to individuals, but to institutions and even nations.[13]

British theologian Lesslie Newbigin, from a different time and location (who also served the cause of the gospel in India), affirmed the same: that the answer to the question "'Who am I?'" can only be given if we ask, "What is my story?," and that can only be answered if there is an answer to the further question, "What is the whole story of which my story is a part?"[14]

Narratives have so much power over us, because they define for us our visions and expectations. They are the grid and lens through which we construe the past and imagine the future, by which we make sense of the present—this moment and this place. They constitute the substructure of who we are, what we know, and our imagination.

In light of narrative as an episteme, text ceases to be primarily about words and meanings attached to them, either by author or context (of the author or reader), but rather, text is considered as the script of the story. Words are given meaning by the story, since both the author and the contexts of the author and readers are essentially stories. Narrative, as the structure for meaning-making, frees us from what Walter Mignolo called "the hegemony of *alphabet-oriented notions of text and discourse*."[15] Social location, meaning-making, and communication are primarily about stories

12. Abbott, *Cambridge Introduction to Narrative*, 1.
13. Katongole, *Sacrifice of Africa*, 2.
14. Newbigin, *Gospel in a Pluralist Society*, 100.
15. Marana et al., 3.

and narratives. Visions and dreams of life are grounded in stories. Those visions and dreams (which constitute our imagination) shape our actions and mis-actions. The spheres of public life, such as culture and religion, economics and politics, social goods and services, arts and entertainment, and the environment, are all a performance of narratives.

However, stories and narratives are not of the same significance. There are stories that are simply accounts of single events or particular locations; but there are also stories that hold together diverse events and locations within one story line; and then there is even a bigger story whose story line integrates many story lines. The latter includes the stories which give structure to our understandings of the world and our location in it, shaping our collective vision of life. They can be identified as "defining narratives," and there are at least three types: (1) those that relate to beginnings, what Katongole calls "founding narratives";[16] (2) narratives of *telos*—purpose, intent, end, or goal, or what N. T. Wright refers to as "controlling narratives";[17] and (3) narratives that capture the entire drama, connecting the founding story with *telos*, what Christopher J. H. Wright calls "grand narrative."[18]

What makes consideration of evangelism practices critical is because it is a performance of all three types of defining narratives. Defining narratives make determination of what reality is; they name the reality we know and the one which we hope for. They are invisible, like the roots that hold the stem, branches, the flowers, and the fruits of a tree. Katongole states, "But if stories are essential to the way we live, they, like the air we breathe, often remains invisible. This does not mean their hold on us is any less powerful. On the contrary, to the extent that the stories that form our imagination remain invisible, they hold us more deeply in their grip."[19] As Barbara Hardy wrote, "We dream in narrative, day-dream in narrative, remember, anticipate, hope, despair, believe, doubt, plan, revise, criticize, construct, gossip, learn, hate and love by narrative. In order really to live, we make up stories about ourselves and others, about the personal as well as the social past and future."[20] Thus, defining narratives create myths; myths create imaginations about the world and a range of possibilities about how

16. Katongole, *Sacrifice of Africa*, 16.

17. Wright, *Challenge of Jesus*, 159.

18. Wright, *Mission of God.*

19. Katongole, *Sacrifice of Africa*, 3.

20. Hardy, "Towards a Poetics of Fiction," 5, which is also quoted in Evans, *Inspired*, 20.

we inhabit it. And, just as narratives symbolize hope, they also form the basis of our fears and traumas.

De-construction, therefore, entails uncovering and interrogating the underlying narratives, which can lead to their re-construction. Narrative is a hermeneutical structure for unearthing the patterns of power embedded in the practice of evangelism. Which better teacher to explicate this than the one who embodies the *evangel*—Jesus of Nazareth, the Christ of God? Luke's account of the episode of the post-resurrection encounter of Jesus and the two disciples on the road to Emmaus offers a paradigm for engaging de-construction and re-construction. It is one of those few anecdotes that covers the contours of the founding, controlling, and grand narratives that constitute the *evangel* and evangelism. The encounter brings to the fore two different defining narratives of messiahship, two different visions and imaginations of God, and two different visions of what God intended for Israel and the world. Essentially, they are two different conceptions of the *evangel* and its power.

Modelling De-Construction: Jesus with the Disciples on the Road to Emmaus (Luke 24:12–35)

When Jesus joins the two disciples, he was the subject of conversation (his tragic and gruesome death on the Roman cross) but the disciples could not recognize him. They even provided the details of the weekend's events, bemused that he should be asking about events that were public news all over Jerusalem. They explained to him that the one who had been condemned as a criminal and subjected to the most humiliating form of execution was the one in whom they had invested their hopes as the promised Messiah: the messenger of God's good news, "a prophet, powerful in word and deed before God and all the people . . . the one who was going to redeem Israel."[21] The fact that it is their chief priests and rulers who handed him over to the Roman authorities to be sentenced to death made it even more unbearable. But how is it possible that the two disciples could not recognize Jesus, the very subject of their conversation? Why could they not recognize the one they had followed for years, heard preach and teach, and observed doing signs and wonders?

21. Luke 24:19–21. All Scripture in this chapter is taken from the New International Version (NIV).

Having witnessed him die (and in the cruel manner in which he was killed), there was no possibility that he could be present with them in any way. Moreover, the possibility that one who has died could come back to life in this world did not exist in their imagination. They had seen Jesus die on the Roman cross, and that ended the story. The expression, "but we had hoped that he was the one who was going to redeem Israel" (Luke 24:21) indicates that, up to the point of his death on the cross, they had hoped that he was the promised Messiah. In order to appreciate why the death on the cross had ended their hopes in Jesus as the Messiah, we need to ponder the narratives that created the disciples' vision and imagination of the nature and character of the Christ they expected.

The Greek word, *Christos* ("Christ" in English), has the same meaning as the Hebrew word, *Mashiach* ("Messiah" in English): "anointed one."[22] In the ancient Near East, kingship was believed to have been lowered from heaven and to have its roots in the original creation and organization of the world. Kings possessed divine office while they lived (understood differently in various times and cultures) and even became gods when they died.[23] Therefore, a king and the nature of his rule were supposed to manifest the divine power he represented, symbolizing social, political-economic, and religious power. Even so, for Israel, the "anointed one," as the coming king, was expected to rule as God's viceroy; literally, a king chosen by God to rule as God would and bring God's salvation for the people and the sovereignty of Israel. The memory of King David, the most famous of all the kings of Israel, created an expectation of a descendant of David who would rule like King David. This imagination was also reinforced in the prophetic image of the Son of Man of Daniel's vision (Daniel 7–8). In instituting God's rule, they believed the Messiah would put right all things, among which was the restoration of Israel's hegemony: conquering all Israel's enemies and re-ordering the world in favor of the cause of Israel; redeeming Israel from a long history of shame and subjugation by foreign empires.

It is in this narrative that they located Jesus of Nazareth, as he performed miracles and prophet-like teaching. It is the story they lived and the narrative that informed their experience of Jesus over the last three years. As N. T. Wright comments,

> They had been living out of a story, a controlling narrative. This story was built up from historical precedents, prophetic promises,

22. Block, "Messiah/Messianism," 503.

23. Walton et al., *IVP Bible Background Commentary*, 291.

> and of course, from the songs of the psalter. The exodus was the backdrop. God's subsequent liberations of his people from various foreign powers formed successive narrative layers pointing in the same direction. When pagan oppression was at its height, Israel's God would step in and deliver her once more. "Why are you so heavy, O my soul? Why so cast down within me? Hope in God—for I will yet praise him, my help and my God."[24]

Thus, the Messiah was supposed to possess superior, coercive force and root out the current impostor—the Roman Empire—and re-establish Israel to its former glory. Accordingly, a Messiah could not possibly suffer and die at the hands of the very force he was supposed to vanquish and bring freedom to God's people. Alas, Jesus of Nazareth had been crushed by the very empire he was to conquer; executed by the very enemies of Israel that he was expected to overthrow. It was not the crucifixion, per se, that was the reason for despondency, because crucifixions were a common occurrence in first-century Rome. The one they had hoped to be the Messiah had been crucified by the very empire he was supposed to root out. Even worse, didn't Moses declare that "anyone who is hung on a pole is under God's curse" (Deut 21:23)? Death on the Roman cross had dashed and obliterated their hopes that Jesus of Nazareth was the Christ-Savior. The imagination and identification of Jesus with Israel's Messiah–king collapsed.

The Messiah the disciples had expected, according to the narrative that created their imagination and hope of his kingly rule, was one who would come with superior power, defeat the Roman imperial powers, and restore the former glory of Jerusalem and Israel as it was in the heydays of King David. It envisioned a world in which Israel was the dominant power, a kind of totalitarianism, with one nationalist vision of the world. The Messiah would possess superior power, conquer and vanquish Israel's enemies, and establish Israel's dominance over all the other nations—an exercise in patterns of power that are characteristic of domination and conquest. Although suffering was part of the prophetic imagination of the promised messiah (for example, in the Suffering Servant in Isaiah 53), over generations—from the time the kingdoms of Israel and Judah were vanquished—a survival narrative emerged that was built on the memory of King David, the great conqueror-king. A system of faith was developed: a conception of God as conqueror on behalf of Israel, a rule of faith anchored within the memory of historical symbols of Jewish identity (temple, land, and

24. Wright, *Challenge of Jesus*, 159.

priesthood). In anticipation of the coming of the warrior-imperial-messiah, communities of protest and survival emerged, such as the Pharisees, Sadducees, and Zealots. While these parties were not in agreement about the nature and character of the expected Messiah, among the ordinary Jewish people, the imperial Savior–Messiah served as the dominant narrative.

On the road to Emmaus, the way Jesus engaged with the two disciples resulted in the de-constructing their defining narratives. First, he let them tell their version of the events of the week, framed within their warrior-conqueror-messiah controlling narrative. Then, he showed them how their narrative was inconsistent with what they purported to be its basis: the Scriptures. His answer to that critical question—"Did not the Messiah have to suffer these things and then enter his glory?"—was a resounding "Yes!" He reproached them for misunderstanding and distorting the Scriptures; and for misperceiving and mis-telling the messianic narrative, showing to them that the crucifixion on the Roman cross was a fulfilment of what was essential to the identity of God's Messiah, "beginning with Moses and all the prophets" (Luke 24:27). He turned the tables on them: "The one who was going to redeem Israel" was attested by suffering on the Roman cross.

Notably, the moment of epiphany is when the "stranger" ate with them. Luke is very deliberate in making this point: thus, their "eyes were opened, and they recognized him" only when he "took bread, gave thanks, broke it and began to give it to them" (Luke 24:30). Jesus wanted them to know that the crucified one was the very one they had believed in; that the one with whom they had dined and followed for three years was the very one promised in the Hebrew Scriptures as the Messiah. Jesus' death on the cross was not the disaster that the disciples thought it was but was integral and central to his messianic calling: the Savior–Christ as a suffering servant. The two, "suffering" and "Christ," are inseparable; suffering is the essential feature of the Christ of the Hebrew Scriptures, "beginning with Moses and all the Prophets . . . in all the scriptures" (Luke 24:27), or otherwise stated as "the Law of Moses, the Prophets, and the Psalms" (Luke 24:44). Therefore, removing the death on the Roman cross from the messianic narrative was tantamount to distorting and misrepresenting Moses and the prophets' vision of the Messiah. It was a distortion and misrepresentation of the nature and character of God, his salvation in and for Israel and the world. Since the Christ is one who rules as God, suffering is the clue to understanding the nature and character of God and the world that God purposed in creation. Suffering and death on the cross were not the evil that had thwarted

God's plans for Israel and the world, but rather, the sign of the inbreaking of God's rule that triumphs over power relations in opposition to God's character, purposes, and plans.

Jesus de-constructed a controlling narrative which centered conquest, domination, and violence, and re-constructed it by centering suffering as the means by which God's rule is inaugurated. In taking upon himself suffering as the Christ, Jesus showed the means and ways of the One with ultimate power who exercises it. Christ's suffering is the re-ordering of power. In suffering violence, the humanity of both the perpetrator and the victim was embraced. Jesus' death on the cross displayed the illusionary nature of narratives of domination and superiority; the real, superior power is the power of love, justice, and holiness displayed in the Christ crucified. Thus, it was only after the disciples recognized that Jesus of Nazareth was the crucified one that he defined their place in the continuing story of God's rule. Luke tells us that "Jesus said to them, 'This is what I told you while I was still with you: Everything must be fulfilled that is written about me in the Law of Moses, the Prophets and the Psalms.' . . . 'Christ will suffer and rise from the dead on the third day, and repentance and forgiveness of sins will be preached in his name to all nations'" (Luke 24:44, 46–47).

Jesus' message is clear to his disciples gathered in Jerusalem: just as the death on the cross and the resurrection defined the good news of God in the Christ, the same cross and resurrection was the kernel of the story to tell the world. According to Jesus, the storyline of Moses, the prophets, and the writings did not only point to the suffering Christ, but the same suffering Christ would be the kernel of the witness of his followers. His disciples were "witnesses of these things" (Luke 24:48); at the heart of which was the crucifixion of Jesus of Nazareth.

Reforming Evangelism: Re-Imagining the *Evangel*

What presents, therefore, the more effective ways and means of communicating the gospel message, taking into account its impact in Africa, in the light of its new celebrated status as the new heartland of Christianity?[25]

25. An observation made, first by world-renowned, Scottish missiologist Andrew Walls in 1982 and later published in his work *Missionary Movement in Christian History*, 9 and *Cross-Cultural Process in Christian History*, 85; and later by Kwame Bediako in *Christianity in Africa* and *Jesus in Africa*, later published as *Jesus and the Gospel in Africa*; and Lamin Sanneh in *Whose Religion Is Christianity?* All three eminent scholars of the global Christian movement affirmed that Africa had now become a new center of

Emmanuel Katongole asserts that "despite the growth of Christianity and the social activism of the churches, Africans are, in general, 40 percent worse off than they were in the 1980s. One then wonders: 'What accounts for the dismal social impact of Christianity in Africa?' 'Why has Christianity, despite its overwhelming presence, failed to make a significant dent in the social history of the continent?'"[26] It became clear, that not only were the founding and controlling narratives of the countries and states of sub-Saharan Africa rooted in colonialism—so was Christianity and the churches.[27]

Unsettling Truths attempts to encapsulate and articulate the inextricable bond between colonialism and missionary evangelization of the new world (read: "Americas, Africa, and Asia").[28] The text draws our attention to the Spanish and Portuguese expeditions at the end of the fifteenth century to Africa and to the Americas—the precursors to the European conquest and introduction of Christianity. It is during this period that the interdependence between colonialism and Christian mission was established—dubbed as "The Age of Discovery," authorized by the Roman pontiff (a period that continued into the early seventeenth century, also known as "The Age of Exploration"), and augmented by "The Doctrine of Discovery" (also by pontiffs of Rome).[29]

Motivated by the push to curtail the further spread of Islam, discovery was implemented to bring the "New World" under the rule of so-called "Christian empires." The Doctrine of Discovery gave the so-called "Christian" monarchies, Spain and Portugal, the "right of conquest, sovereignty, and dominance over non-Christian peoples, along with their lands, territories, and resources."[30] The template of patterns of power and power relations between the conqueror and the conquered was written, creating "social hierarchies; economic, racial, and sexual inequality; economic and cultural dependency."[31] Part of the mandate was to ensure conversion to

---

gravity of Christianity and predicted that African Christianity would be the representative Christianity of the twenty-first century.

26. Katongole, *Sacrifice of Africa*, 40.

27. I draw from my paper, presented to the Africa Society for Evangelical Theology Conference in Nairobi, March 2023; see Niringiye, "On this Rock I will Build My Church."

28. Charles and Rah, *Unsettling Truths*.

29. Charles and Rah, *Unsettling Truths*.

30. Frichner, "Impact on Indigenous Peoples," 7–8.

31. Marana et al., *Coloniality at Large*, 9.

Christianity by any means, including coercion, slavery, and extermination of those who resisted conquest and conversion. The name for this assignment was "mission." It was "the tool of empire—whose effectiveness depended upon a complex ontology of non-European human beings. This ontology simultaneously affirmed the humanity and subjectivity of Natives, albeit in diminished or infantilized way, and denied their humanity and objectified them as savages and beasts."[32]

The process of the evangelization of sub-Saharan Africa by missionaries from Europe and North America in the eighteenth century followed the same patterns of power, domination, and conquest embedded in colonialism. Arguably, the same patterns typify current models and methods, not only in the West, but also by the churches which were either planted or have emerged over the last five centuries. There are exceptions to this rule, but as the axiom goes, "Exceptions prove the rule."

It is not surprising that the churches which were a result of that evangelization were conceived as extensions of those based in Europe and North America with the same denominational church polity. The Roman Catholic Church and the variety of Western Protestant churches (such as Anglican, Lutheran, Presbyterian, Methodist, and Baptist) enjoyed the favor of the colonial governments and assured them of numerical strength. Today's Catholic and Protestant churches constitute the majority of Christian expression on the continent—standing at about 50 percent of the total Christian population in Africa in 2010.[33]

Katongole names the challenge of Christianity in Africa as the product of evangelism. It "cannot provide the critical challenge to the political and economic illusions of a postcolonial Africa," because it "nicely locates itself within the dominant imagination of postcolonial politics and economics in Africa and quite often reproduces its patterns, its modernity, and its illusory promises of success and prosperity."[34] Sub-Saharan Africa gives evidence of the resounding success of modern-day practices of evangelism and provides a compelling case for the urgent need to de-construct its underlying founding and controlling narratives.

The primary captivity of expressions of evangelism is not to culture, but rather, to empire. The patterns of power performed in Christian evangelism are the same as those of empire. The necessary de-construction of

32. Ray, "Doctrine of Discovery," 82, and quoted in Green, "Death of Mission."

33. Mandryk, *Operation World*, 32.

34. Katongole, *Sacrifice of Africa*, 49, 50.

these defining narratives, as Jesus did in his encounter with two disciples on the road to Emmaus, may actually lead to a categorical rejection of some of the old models. These models not only misrepresent the gospel, but they are a performance of the patterns of power that propel injustice, exploitation, and violence. Renouncing these models portends freedom from the very power patterns they perform, releasing us to re-imagine new models that embody and commend the *evangel* of God's love, justice, and peace in Jesus, the Christ. Evangelism ceases to be a performance of mission, but rather, of bearing witness by the power of the Holy Spirit, as Jesus promised his disciples.

Bibliography

Abbott, H. Porter. *The Cambridge Introduction to Narrative*. Cambridge: Cambridge University Press, 2002.

Bediako, Kwame. *Christianity in Africa: The Renewal of a Non-Western Religion*. Maryknoll, NY: Orbis, 1995.

———. *Jesus and the Gospel in Africa: History and Experience*. Theology in Africa Series. Maryknoll, NY: Orbis, 2004.

Berger, Peter, and Thomas Luckmann. *The Social Construction of Reality: A Treatise in the Sociology of Knowledge*. Garden City, NY: Doubleday, 1966.

Block, Daniel L. "Messiah/Messianism." In *Dictionary for Theological Interpretation of the Bible*, edited by Kevin J. Vanhoozer et al., 503–6. Grand Rapids: Baker Academic, 2005.

Bright, Bill. *Have You Heard of the Four Spiritual Laws?* Orlando: Campus Crusade for Christ, 2007.

Charles, Mark, and Soong-Chan Rah. *Unsettling Truths: The Ongoing, Dehumanizing Legacy of the Doctrine of Discovery*. Downers Grove, IL: InterVarsity, 2019.

Derrida, Jacques. *Writing and Difference*. Translated by Alan Bass. Chicago: University of Chicago Press, 1978.

Evans, Rachel Held. *Inspired: Slaying Giants, Walking on Water, and Loving the Bible*. Nashville: Nelson, 2018.

Frichner, Tonya Gonnella. "Impact on Indigenous Peoples of the International Legal Construct Known as the Doctrine of Discovery, Which Has Served as the Foundation of the Violation of their Human Rights." A Preliminary Study presented at the United Nations' Economic and Social Council's Permanent Forum on Indigenous Issues, Ninth Session, New York, April 19–20, 2010. www.un.org/esa/socdev/unpfii/documents/E%20C.19%202010%2013.DOC.

Green, Gene L. "The Death of Mission: Rethinking the Great Commission." *Journal of NAIITS* 12 (2014) 81–110.

Grenz, Stanley J. *A Primer on Postmodernism*. Grand Rapids: Eerdmans, 1996.

Hardy, Barbara. "Towards a Poetics of Fiction: An Approach Through Narrative." *NOVEL: A Forum on Fiction* 2 (1968) 5–14.

Katongole, Emmanuel. *The Sacrifice of Africa: A Political Theology for Africa.* Grand Rapids: Eerdmans, 2011.

Mandryk, Jason. *Operation World: The Definitive Prayer Guide to Every Nation.* 7th ed. Downers Grove, IL: InterVarsity, 2010.

Maraña, Mabel, et al., eds. *Coloniality at Large: Latin America and the Postcolonial Debate.* Durham, NC: Duke University Press, 2008.

McDowell, Josh, and Sean McDowell. *Evidence That Demands a Verdict: Life-Changing Truth for a Skeptical World.* Rev. ed. Nashville: Thomas Nelson, 2017.

Mott, Stephen Charles. *Biblical Ethics and Social Change.* 2nd ed. New York: Oxford University Press, 2011.

Newbigin, Lesslie. *The Gospel in a Pluralist Society.* Grand Rapids: Eerdmans, 1989.

Niringiye, David Zac. "On this Rock I will Build My Church: Ecclesiology in Africa." Paper presented at the Africa Society for Evangelical Theology Conference, Nairobi, March 2023.

Prior, Karen Swallow. *The Evangelical Imagination: How Stories, Images, and Metaphors Created a Culture in Crisis.* Grand Rapids: Brazos, 2023.

Rah, Soong-Chan. *The Next Evangelicalism: Freeing the Church from Western Cultural Captivity.* Downers Grove, IL: InterVarsity, 2009.

Ray, Alan. "The Doctrine of Discovery and the Conquest of the Americas." Speech presented at Wheaton College, Wheaton, IL, October 1, 2012.

Sanneh, Lamin. *Whose Religion Is Christianity? The Gospel Beyond the West.* Grand Rapids: Eerdmans, 2003.

Walls, Andrew. *The Cross-Cultural Process in Christian History.* Maryknoll, NY: Orbis, 2002.

———. *The Missionary Movement in Christian History: Studies in the Transmission of Faith.* Maryknoll, NY: Orbis, 1996.

Walton, John H., et al. *The IVP Bible Background Commentary: Old Testament.* Downers Grove, IL: IVP Academic, 2000.

Wright, Christopher J. H. *The Mission of God: Unlocking the Bible's Grand Narrative.* Downers Grove, IL: InterVarsity, 2006.

Wright, N. T. *The Challenge of Jesus: Rediscovering Who Jesus Was and Is.* Downers Grove, IL: InterVarsity, 1999.

Chapter 2

God-Gifted Interruptions

The Power of God's Liberating Good News Is Displayed in the Midst of the Unexpected

Ruth Padilla DeBorst

Infatuated. In love with numbers, percentages, rates of adoption, progress scales. Imprisoned by the spirit of globalized marketing. Consumer ratings populate the imaginary of many a church and parachurch agency. Add to the mix a good dose of illusions of power and conquest, and you get the perfect evangelistic recipe: Seven simple steps for taking over the world for Christ. How to conquer the world. Winning the world for Christ. Evangelism marketing experts. End times promotion. Strategies and formulas, statistics, and pragmatic plans—all are devised to guarantee success in the evangelistic venture. Today's passage throws this entire paradigm into question and challenges us to welcome God-gifted interruptions as witnesses of the Spirit's transformative power, not our own.

Now, before digging into our topic, two other matters: First, in true Latin American fashion, I must bring you greetings. Greetings from your sisters and brothers at Casa Adobe, the intentional Christian community to which my husband, James, and I belong in Costa Rica. In this community composed of several families, including refugees, we are seeking to live the good news: being the church Monday through Sunday and being good neighbors to our human and non-human neighbors. Second, we cannot ponder the good news in this conference without painfully acknowledging all that is *not* good news in our world today. I invite you to a moment of silent prayer in favor of the people of Palestine and Israel, mourning the loss of life and begging for a cessation to violence . . . Lord, have mercy!

They had recently made new friends, who had responded positively to their ministry: Paul, Silas, and Doctor Luke were warmly welcomed into the home of a well-off Greek businesswoman. Lydia, along with the members of her household, had been baptized in the city of Philippi after they had received and accepted the good news of Jesus Christ.[1] I can imagine it was not too easy for Paul and his companions to overcome their cultural prejudices regarding the leadership of women in the new community of the Way, but they appear to have made peace with the situation, so accompanying this budding community of gentile Christ-followers seemed to be the logical next step for the itinerant missionaries. Consequently, the plan for that day was to join the women by the river. This would be another opportunity to help deepen the faith of these new believers.

But something—or rather someone, whose life contrasted significantly with that of Lydia—interrupted them.

"These men, who serve the One Above Us All, are showing us the way to be set free and made whole."[2]

Truly, this was not the first time the oppressed slave girl had shouted this out as she followed Paul and the others around. She had been doing so for days and days, and it was obvious that she was under the influence of a powerful spirit. Perhaps it was her insistence, the unhelpful public exposure, the knowledge that she was being sorely exploited, or simple frustration at the interruption that moved a troubled Paul to order the spirit, "As one who represents Creator Sets Free (Jesus), the Chosen One, I tell you now to come out of this woman!"[3] Right away, the spirit left her, says Luke.[4]

Far outside of Paul's neat plan, God's Spirit intervened, and the girl was freed from at least one of her oppressors. The power of God's liberating good news was displayed in the midst of the unexpected to all whose eyes were not blocked by self-interest or prejudice.

But the story did not end there, with Paul and his friends walking on to carry out their plans. The interruption became yet more complicated as the plot thickened. Prodded by the disgruntled exploiters who capitalized

1. Acts 16:13–15. All Scripture quotations in this sermon are from the First Nations Version (FNV).

2. Acts 16:17.

3. Acts 16:18.

4. Acts 16:19.

on the popular prejudice towards outsiders in this prominent Roman colony, the crowd attacked Paul and Silas, who were stripped, beaten, and thrown into prison under extreme measures.[5] Things were most definitely not going as planned!

Even less planned was the violent earthquake that shook the prison and loosened everyone's chains. And totally unexpected were the posture and actions of the jailer, who fell trembling before Paul and Silas and begged, "What must I do to be set free and made whole?"[6]

He had already been saved from his own sword; but the witness of the disciples awoke a thirst for a deeper, fuller salvation. And they were prompt to share Creator's good story.

"Put your trust in Creator Sets Free (Jesus), our Honored Chief," they said to him. "He will make you whole and set you and all your family free *to follow him*."[7]

How long they spoke we do not know, but again, as in the case of Lydia, the whole household was baptized, and this retired Roman soldier joyfully opened his home to Paul and Silas.[8] Imagine what it must have felt like to them! Just hours before, this very man had roughly clamped down their feet into the prison stocks. And here he was, washing their wounds and offering them food, surrounded by his family, in his home! Again, God's liberating good news was displayed in the midst of the unexpected. But this time, it was Paul and Silas who were on the *receiving* end, as the jailer witnessed through his radical hospitality to the transformative power of the Evangel. Imagine that: the messenger learning from the recipient of the message! I, for one, wish Luke had told us more about the life of this jailer after his baptism, and I would have loved to hear the voice of his wife and the rest of the family. However, it is not a stretch to think that the unnamed jailer would have had to reconsider his occupation, or, at least, the way he carried it out as he stepped into the plot of a story that relativized imperial power, equalized all relationships, and called people to serve instead of being served.

After this, Paul and Silas were finally freed, and the magistrates begged them to leave the city once they realized they were Roman citizens and could denounce them for mistreatment. As soon as they were released—Luke

5. Acts 16:19–24.

6. Acts 16:30.

7. Acts 16:31; emphasis added.

8. Acts 16:32–34.

finishes off the story of those accidented twenty-four hours—they went back to Lydia's house, where they met with their siblings in the faith and encouraged them. As they traveled on from Philippi, they left behind a very unlikely community of believers: among others, a Greek entrepreneur, a bunch of women, a Roman jailer, and his family.[9]

I propose to you that the road of life and ministry as people of the Way is filled with God-gifted interruptions. We may not be called to cast out a demon or to free a jailer from suicide. But, as participants in Creator's story of good purposes for the entire creation, we all need to be attentive to the opportunities God sends our way to serve as channels of God's saving grace, even when these upset our best-laid plans. And, at the same time, we need to be open to *receiving* the good news from unexpected people, in unexpected places, in unexpected ways. God-gifted interruptions, are we open to them?

We might, for example, be heading to our desk to prepare a sermon, when we get a call from a person in need of a hearing ear. We might be focusing our attention on our seminary students when a migrant family shows up on campus. We might be about to leave for church when a neighbor knocks on our door. We might be so wrapped up in our own agendas that we become unaware of our personal and communal complicity in systems of oppression and blinded to our need to change course. We might be so engaged in the rituals of religion that we are numbed to the cry of the people and the cry of the earth. God-gifted interruptions, are we open to them?

The path of the scholar, researcher, teacher, pastor, leader is thickly paved with obligations and responsibilities: academic, pastoral, familial. And we can get so absorbed in our work that we grow calloused to the realities of people around us and deaf to the stirring of God's Spirit, who may be calling us off our expected course or seeking to convert *us*. God-gifted interruptions, are we open to them? Do we believe enough in the power of the gospel that we are ready to serve as witnesses in word and deed of the wondrous and liberating acts of God, even when this might draw us away from our neatly pre-established agendas? Are we sufficiently aware of our own, constant need for humility and course correction?

Luke's retelling of those twenty-four hours in the life of Paul and Silas is recorded in Acts as a steady reminder of the power of the gospel. Power to deliver from evil forces. Power to transform social relations and

9. Acts 16:35–40.

bring justice. Power to transcend limitations of all sorts. Power to free from death. Power to restore relationships and generate new communities out of people as unlikely as a Greek businesswoman and a Roman jailer, who are counted among the founders of the church in Philippi.

It is my prayer that, as we continue living into God's story, we might remain open to the promptings of God's Spirit, so that we may welcome the God-gifted interruptions that come our way. May we release our infatuation with strategies, numbers, and control and, instead, surrender to the Spirit with humility, proclaiming, demonstrating, celebrating, and being radically transformed by the power of the good news!

Chapter 3

Global Evangelism

Vinoth Ramachandra

Let me begin with a word of personal testimony: I am grateful that I became a Christian, not by hearing an evangelist inviting me to respond to a set of doctrinal propositions called "the gospel," but rather, by reading the accounts of Jesus of Nazareth in the New Testament and simply "falling in love" with the figure presented there. What first attracted me was his sparkling wit, expressed in aphorisms and parables, and so often directed at the "religious types" that I was familiar with (and repelled by) in Sri Lanka. He was constantly provoking the religious establishment by the way he trampled all over their pious conventions and traditions. I loved the way he was gentle towards the weak and vulnerable, and scathing—even harsh—in his criticism of the powerbrokers of his society. I wanted to know him and serve him with my life, and so I was confirmed in the Anglican church in Colombo just before my eighteenth birthday.

It is because the good news was, for me, a person—Jesus of Nazareth—that I have never understood the acrimonious squabbles that have marked the so-called Evangelical churches over whether "evangelism" or "social action" is primary in the mission of the church. When I look at Jesus, the same action can, from one point of view, be regarded as "evangelism" (say, presenting himself as the Messiah to the Samaritan woman); from another perspective, it is radical political action (trampling down the barriers between men and women, Jews and Samaritans). I see Jesus healing the sick, casting out demons, befriending the outcasts, forgiving sinners, loving his enemies, and preaching the arrival of God's kingdom to the poor.

In fact, the noun "evangelism" is found nowhere in the New Testament. Nor do we find terms such as "social action" or "social responsibility." They are foreign to the thinking of the early church. When the first Christians went around the garbage heaps of Roman cities picking up babies left to die and bringing them up in their homes, or when they refused to fight in Caesar's armies, or when they built shelters for the poor, cared for the sick and enemy prisoners of war, they were not discharging something they called their "social responsibility." No; they were simply living out the gospel. If God had come to us in the form of a human servant embracing the vulnerability, shame, and suffering of others; then embracing the vulnerability, shame, and suffering of others was the divine—and also truly human—way to live. In fact, Ignatius of Antioch regarded it as one of the marks of the heretics of his day that they "had no thought for the widow and orphan, none at all for the afflicted. The captive, the hungry, or the thirsty."[1]

Still in Thrall to Christendom?

> How has it come about that the development of Christianity and the church has given birth to a society, a culture that are completely opposite to what we read in the Bible? . . . There is not just deviation but radical and essential contradiction, or real subversion.[2]

The late French sociologist Jacques Ellul obviously exaggerates in his desire to provoke self-scrutiny. After all, a growing body of scholarship has shown how so much that the modern, "secular" West takes for granted and reveres—experimental science, liberal democracy, constitutionalism, universal human rights, the social welfare state, and even secularism itself—are the fruit of Christian history.[3] But these ideas and practices were the work of a few gifted, theologically literate intellectuals. And they were all also opposed by others within Christendom. So Ellul's words need to be pondered by all who take Christian mission seriously. Our missionary passion is a fruit of the Holy Spirit's energizing influence in the church and in our personal lives. If we are convinced that the Creator God is like Jesus, and that evil and death do not have the last word because of the cross–resurrection,

1. Ignatius of Antioch, "Epistle to the Smyrnaeans," chap. 6.

2. Ellul, *Subversion of Christianity*, 3.

3. See, especially, Holland, *Dominion*. Also, Taylor, *Secular Age*; O'Donovan, *Desire of the Nations*.

communicating that joyful news is natural. But our passion must be tempered by sober attention to the ambivalent legacy of Western Christendom and the sociological and political dimensions of faith. As the old adage goes, "Those who ignore the mistakes of history are condemned to repeat them."

But Ellul goes on to make an even more shocking statement: "Christendom has astutely abolished Christianity by making us all Christians. . . . In Christendom there is not the slightest idea of what Christianity is. *People cannot understand that Christianity has been abolished by its propagation.*"[4]

This paradox is rarely reflected upon by Evangelical church leaders. We desire that the gospel be proclaimed to every human being and that all should come to know Jesus as Lord. But what if our prayers are answered? What will that Christian confession involve in a society where there are no more any *fundamental* differences among us? And will those who come after us have any idea of what it means to be a "Christian" if there are no "non-Christians" among them?

Of course, we know that not everybody, perhaps not even the majority of our fellow citizens, will become Christians. The day when kings and tribal chiefs were converted, and the whole nation or tribe became Christian (and were subjected to mass baptisms and catechisms)—that day is long past and most probably will never return. But does such realism prompt lament and social withdrawal, or does it become an opportunity for developing new paradigms of post-Christian mission in the West?

It is salutary to recall that Christianity began as a narrative from the margins. Jesus was born outside Bethlehem, escaped as a refugee to Egypt, spent his life as an itinerant homeless preacher in an obscure province of the Roman Empire, and ended his life on a Roman cross outside the walls of Jerusalem.

For the early Christians in the Roman Empire, the temptation to withdraw from society must have been extremely powerful. They worshiped a Savior who had been executed as an insurgent against the state. They had no illusions about the *Pax Romana*, or that the ruling regime represented a sacred order that was above critique. They saw themselves as belonging to a *third race*, comprising believing Jews and gentiles—nothing less than the firstfruits of a new humanity, authorized and governed directly by the risen Christ. This multinational community, and not their particular *civitas*, claimed their ultimate loyalty. Some of them may have been citizens of Rome, but their primary citizenship was elsewhere (Phil 3:20). However,

4. Ellul, *Subversion of Christianity*, 36–37; emphasis added.

since they were not competing with the state for territorial control, they could pay their taxes and discharge other civic duties.

The political theologian Michael Budde comments, "The idea that one could 'change' one's race or ethnicity seems impossible in a culture in which these are the quintessential ascriptive identities, largely unchangeable or immutable; for us, on the other hand, 'religion' is a voluntary, changeable, and fluid part of identity, since one can 'change' religions. But for Christianity in the early centuries, becoming part of the Christian 'race' or ethnic community was available to all regardless of their communities or identities of origin—'conversion' was the process of changing races, of joining the peoplehood of Christ."[5]

Here are a couple of representative quotes from two prominent European Christian thinkers of the early twentieth century that should further cause us to pause from our unreflective activism.

Emil Brunner (1889–1966): "That the church turned so much toward doctrine, so little toward discipleship, is a chief reason for its weakness, which is now becoming apparent. A church that detaches itself from the world only in speaking, even if it were speaking in the purest Biblical doctrine, but not in action and love, becomes unworthy of belief to the world."[6]

Dietrich Bonhoeffer (1906–1945): "We justified the world and condemned as heretics those who tried to follow Christ. The result was that a nation became Christian and Lutheran, but at the cost of true discipleship . . . the call to follow Jesus in the narrow way was hardly ever heard."[7]

In a different context, the Filipina anthropologist and theologian Melba Maggay bemoans the fact that, although the Philippines has had almost five centuries of Christian tradition as brought by Spanish and American colonizers, and is reputed to be the "only Christian nation in the Far East," its "level of corruption shames the name of Christ." "Public justice and social equity is far below that of Buddhist countries in the region. The country's adaptive power is such that it has readily embraced and accommodated the faith of its colonizers, but its deeper substructures have remained unchanged."[8]

5. Budde, *Foolishness to the Gentiles*, 195.

6. Brunner, *Truth as Encounter*, 198.

7. Bonhoeffer, *Cost of Discipleship*, 58.

8. Maggay, "World in Which We Serve."

Unlearning the Gospel

If we are seized by a vision of the coherence of "all things" in Christ (Col. 1:16, 17)[9] and God's eternal purpose to "reconcile" (Col. 1:20, Gk. *apokatallassein*) or "gather up all things" (Eph. 1:10, Gk. *anakephalein*) in Christ, then we cannot be content with an understanding of mission as only bringing as many people as possible to profess a personal faith in Christ. With such a broader understanding of the good news, what we label "evangelism" now becomes, in the words of the late South African missiologist David Bosch, "enlisting people for the reign of God, liberating them from themselves, their sins, and their entanglements, so that they will be free for God and neighbor . . . To win people to Jesus is to win their allegiance to God's priorities."[10]

Therefore, the most urgent need we face is to "unlearn" the gospel as we have received it in many of our churches, both North and South. The gospel is not primarily about *my* needs and how God can satisfy them. It is rather *about the world*. The gospel announces that God has put into effect—through Jesus of Nazareth—his intention to heal, recreate, and reconcile this hurting and fractured world to himself. Furthermore, it is precisely because it is *about* the world's future that the gospel is *for* the world. While I am called to respond personally to that message, the content of that message is far bigger than myself.

For whom is such a message "good news"? For those who yearn for a different world, who have no stake at all in the present idolatrous and oppressive world-system. In Mary's Song (the Magnificat), the mother of our Lord celebrates the coming of "God my Savior" (Luke 1:47) and spells out the implications of his saving rule: scattering the proud in the imagination of their hearts, pulling down the powerful from their thrones, filling the hungry with good things and sending the rich empty away (vv. 51–53). Evidently, the Lucan understanding of Messianic salvation was very "this-worldly"; it was certainly *more* than social reversal or political transformation; but, equally certainly, not *less*.

Little wonder, then, that those who opposed the coming of God's saving rule in the ministry of Jesus were those who benefited from the status quo (for instance, the rich, the socially powerful, and the religious

9. The Scripture translation referenced throughout this chapter is the New Revised Standard Version (NRSV).

10. Bosch, *Transforming Mission*, 418.

leadership), while those who received him—and for whom his message was good news—were those excluded from salvation, as defined by the former. It is interesting that Jesus never insists that such folk (for instance: tax-collectors, lepers, Samaritans, and prostitutes) must first change before they can experience his salvation—not because they had no personal sin, but because they needed no reminders of their moral failures. To such people, he simply opens his arms in forgiveness and unconditional acceptance. Tax collectors, such as Zacchaeus, are so shocked by the generosity of Jesus that they respond spontaneously in repentance. To whom does Jesus directly preach repentance and the need for "new birth"[11] (or, alternatively, to "become like little children")[12] if they are to receive the kingdom of God? To the "pious," who were assured that their seats in the kingdom were already booked; to the rich, whose riches isolated them from God and their fellow men and women; and to the powerful, to whom Jesus' way of humble service towards those at the bottom of society was a threat to their own power-base and their privileged positions.

An Engaged Pluralism

The retreat of Christianity from the center of modern, Western public life is viewed with nostalgia and even paranoia by those Christians who have benefited from the positions of privilege their forebears enjoyed in former ages. But it is welcomed by those minority Christians and the many non-Christians who experienced the dark, oppressive side of European Christendom; or the blatant hypocrisies of an American Christianity which offered little more than a suffocating moralism and served as chaplain to the American empire from the days of its founding.

What should characterize the church, then, if the mushrooming religious and cultural pluralism has now liberated Western Christians to engage in mission from the margins? How can it resist being co-opted once again to serve the political and economic interests of the dominant class? Living as a minority among other minorities, what Christians should ultimately bring to society is a radical love for the stranger and a hospitality and generosity towards those who are different—all of which need to be translated into relevant social and political practices.

11. John 3:3–8.

12. Matt 18:3–4.

The incarnation of the Son/Word of God in human flesh speaks of identification, dependence, vulnerability, and weakness. It proclaims a Savior who comes to us where we are, looks through our eyes, speaks with our tongues, wears our clothes, carries our infirmities, and suffers in solidarity with us. To be incarnational implies that we are fully part of the life of our nations, seeking to understand their dominant ethos and ideologies, being sensitive to their changing contexts, and being fully relational in all that we say and do. Indeed, the authentic missionary experience is to live by the terms set by the "other"—the culture/society that the missionary enters—so that all that is good, true, and beautiful in the "other" can now be given a new direction (namely, towards Christ's kingdom); and all that is contrary to Christ's kingdom can be courageously critiqued and resisted.

Unfortunately, what is called "evangelism" is often reduced to a special, church-based program. The dominant assumption is that evangelism is about inviting non-Christians to come to *our* meetings, to answer *our* questions, to learn *our* language. We are always in control. But such methods, which are always imported from affluent Western churches, mostly reach nominal Christians and a few on the fringes of the church. It leaves those who are not consciously "seeking" (the vast majority) untouched. Moreover, such methods are mindlessly imitative of Western churches that are themselves hopelessly ineffectual in impacting their own societies.

The Singaporean theologian Mark Chan bemoans the fact that "packaged programs proliferate as pastors and churches around the world ape or re-engineer themselves after the image of large churches featured in the popular Christian media."[13] He points out that so many mega-churches are "remarkably alike in that the same standardized programs and approaches are found in them, from authoritative (and sometimes authoritarian) leadership, to structuring the church around cell-groups, to worship-leading styles, to running a church-based Bible school."[14]

How far removed this is from the Jesus we meet in the gospel narratives: a Jesus who is deeply affected by the people and situations he encounters. He asks questions of people, perhaps more than he gives answers, and is surprised by the answers he receives and the unexpected behavior of people he meets. He does not come with ready-made formulas but speaks a particular word to particular people. He teaches his disciples no techniques or methods, save to love people and to be willing to die to self-centered

13. Chan, "Cross Between," 125.

14. Chan, "Cross Between," 125.

ambition. He unashamedly intrudes into conversations started by others and then steers those conversations in a deeper direction (e.g., Luke 24:13 ff).

Christians should likewise be immersing themselves, boldly yet humbly, in those conversations which are taking place in secular workplaces and the public arena (which, for the most part, they have not initiated) and taking them in a different direction. I believe it is possible to start with any subject, from the most ridiculous (even obscene or sacrilegious) to the sublime, and if we ask probing questions, we come down to the bedrock issues that the gospel addresses: What is humanness? What is the nature of ultimate reality? Whence do we derive our values of good and evil, reason, or justice? And so on. Even if we do not succeed in drawing people to personal faith in Christ, we are bearing witness to God's intention to "gather up" all our human activities—whether in the sciences, business, technology, government, and the arts—into Christ (cf. Col 1:15–20). We do not "take Christ" into these conversations; it is he who draws us in. The church needs the discernment to discover Christ in these conversations and activities, and then to articulate his presence with courage, clarity, and relevance.

Thus, an incarnational approach to mission is always *dialogical.* The opposite of a dialogue is a monologue. In dialogue, unlike in monologue, we take risks. We expose ourselves to the full weight of alien, even anti-Christian, thought as well as receiving new truths that enrich our understanding of God and God's world. This means that we must be prepared to listen with attention to people, to listen as well as speak, and indeed, to listen well before we speak. This is the way of friendship and the cultivation of mutual trust and receptivity. It is only in relationships of mutual trust that we can understand each other and speak truthfully in love.

All interreligious encounter is dependent on historical, social, and political context. The dialogue between, say, Buddhists and Christians in Los Angeles will be profoundly different to that between the same groups in Sri Lanka, where Buddhism and politics have long been intertwined; and that latter encounter, again, would be very different in Japan. It is why I find most books on "religious pluralism" or "a theology of religions" quite dissatisfying. They tend to treat "religions" as abstract intellectual systems or worldviews, ignoring the way these traditions and communities have been shaped and transformed by different historical circumstances.

My lifelong exposure to religious communities in Asia (Hindu, Buddhist, Muslim, Confucianist, and Christian) has led me to believe that the vast majority of these communities have a *functional* understanding of their traditions: they are useful for meeting various felt needs, serving as rites of passage, or providing sources of consolation in periods of bereavement, calamity, or national tragedy. The intellectual systems may carry some startling insights and sophisticated logical arguments; their rites and ceremonies may evince moments of great beauty and tenderness; but on the popular level, they are rife with superstition and gullibility, self-righteousness, and oppression.

Peter Cotterell, a theological educator who also served for many years as a Christian missionary in Ethiopia, laments the "hopeless idealization" of religions in many academic discussions: "The horrors of Canaanite religions are still with us, the *shaman* still claims the power to manipulate his gods, witchcraft still flourishes, the credulous are exploited, human achievement is exalted, the rich are filled with yet more good things, and it is the poor who are sent empty away."[15]

What a person really believes and treasures in life can only be discovered through personal engagement. Often, many in Asia who are labeled Buddhists have more in common with primal religionists than with the rationalism of Theravadin scholars or the mysticism of the Mahayanists. Much urban Buddhism is centered on popular Hindu gurus and personal astrologers. Willingness to explore the sacred texts of the religious traditions of others is, of course, a necessary aspect of showing respect; but this can never be a substitute for the more costly demands of friendship. As an old Chinese proverb reminds us, "He who comes with the odor of enmity will invite the clash of weapons, he who comes with the fragrance of friendship will be loved like a brother."[16]

The idea of dialogue often conjures up images of religious dignitaries seated around a table in a set-piece consultation on some esoteric theological topic. While there is a place for such dialogue, especially where these dignitaries represent their respective religious communities, it would be unfortunate if this was taken to be the normal mode of dialogue. I myself have little enthusiasm for such set-piece formal events and am more enthusiastic about informal gatherings of Christians with non-Christians to discuss issues that affect their common life in society.

Christians, in the course of their daily lives, interact and collaborate with non-Christians on social projects of various kinds, from a housing association committee to a government policy think-tank. This is the normal

15. Cotterell, *Mission and Meaninglessness*, 51.

16. Quoted in Needham, *Within the Four Seas*, 159.

context in which opportunities for serious dialogue emerge. It is often in the course of such discussions that questions can be raised that take the discussion onto a more searching, personal level, where peoples' worldviews are disclosed and the basic assumptions on which they conduct their lives open to scrutiny and loving critique.

Cyberspace, which is today's equivalent of the dense network of roads in the Roman Empire, which facilitated the communication of the gospel by the apostles and their emissaries, opens up unique and unprecedented opportunities for inter-religious conversations among individuals and communities who may never encounter each other (for various reasons) in physical space. Although the incarnational aspects of dialogue are subdued by the medium, personal stories can be shared and genuine friendships developed in cyberspace. Christians can also join online campaigns started by others to highlight specific injustices and effect sociopolitical transformation.

As is well known, however, the potential for deception, incivility, and manipulation are also rife on social media. Even where these may be absent, the scholar of Islam Evelyne Reisacher notes that communication-at-a-distance heightens the risks of misunderstanding those whose lives we do not share: "I believe that online cross-cultural and interfaith connections require even greater skill than real-life connections. I am dreaming of required classes in intercultural and interfaith studies for all internet users (who would get their license to access the internet only after passing specific tests on culture)."[17]

Dialogue is not primarily an event, but an attitude—indeed, a way of life. It is a disposition that reaches out and makes room for people who are different or even antagonistic. Understood and practiced as an intentional lifestyle, it goes far beyond mere coexistence or uncritical friendliness. Even in countries where there are legal sanctions against conversion of members of the majority religious group, nobody can prevent people from engaging in personal conversations about their heart-felt convictions.

17. Reisacher, *Joyful Witness*, 56. Reisacher also notes the overwhelming volume of information on the internet that makes it difficult to navigate for the novice: "If I were not a scholar of Islam, I would have no idea how to make sense of all the resources available online. As I now daily surf the web for information on Islam, I have learned to bookmark not only scholarly sites but also sites linked with knowledgeable and influential people, to seek online peer-reviews, to listen to conversations among Muslims, and to highlight recurring questions Muslims are asking." Reisacher, *Joyful Witness*, 51.

Criticizing people's beliefs (though with sympathetic understanding and gentleness, not arrogance) is also to take them seriously. To refuse to criticize the other, or to treat the other as just another version of myself, is to insult the other. (It is, ironically, a rejection of real pluralism!) And we have also insulated ourselves from the possibility of being converted, either to their beliefs or to a deeper understanding of our own. To elevate the similarities and to belittle the fundamental differences between our beliefs and others' is not to take them seriously at all. It is also to betray our own heritage.

The church does not face the world with the claim "We possess the truth; come and learn from us" but rather with the words of witness: "*He* is the truth; come with us to learn from him." This is a posture of bold humility. It is an invitation and a challenge to the world to turn from pseudo-deities and join us in a continual pilgrimage of discovery. Christ "belongs to us only because he belongs to all. He is ours only by virtue of his universality."[18] The church, in turn, needs to be open to the critique of alien secular and religious traditions in order to understand more fully, and obey more deeply, the message with which it has been entrusted. Receiving the gospel is the beginning, not the end, of a journey; it is as if a door has been opened that beckons us into a new world.

The Changing Christian Landscape

The twentieth century was a period of extraordinary sustained Christian growth in sub-Saharan Africa and parts of Asia. Yet, it also witnessed a serious recession from Christian faith in most of Europe, Australasia, and parts of North America; intensified opposition to Christianity in the Islamic world and in most of the Indian subcontinent; and a tragic exodus of Christians from those parts of North Africa and the Middle East that had once been the heartlands of Christianity. In his monumental survey of twentieth-century Christianity, Brian Stanley observes, "Whether or not it can be accurately deemed to be 'the Christian century,' the twentieth century can properly be denominated as the great century of conversion to Christianity. It was necessarily, therefore, a period that also witnessed a radical pluralization of popular understandings of Christianity as the word

18. Cragg, *Call of the Minaret*, 168.

of the gospel took flesh in innumerable cultural forms in non-Western societies."[19]

Just a hundred or so years ago, our village was the world. Now, the world has become our village. Stanley notes that, even as religious pluralism and secularism displaced Christianity from the center of social life in northern-hemisphere cities at the same time, the great migration movements of the past century both diversified and even strengthened the Christian presence there. "Although migrant churches had very limited impact outside their own ethnic constituency, it remains the case that, without such migration flows, the process of recession from Christianity in northern societies over the last century would have been far more marked, not less so."[20]

Often these mono-ethnic churches are the result of insecurity: they serve a cultural, rather than explicitly religious, purpose; but their insecurity is compounded by the insularity of the native "white" churches which have no tradition of hospitality towards strangers (unlike the early church), and even towards fellow Christians who have different colored skin or speak a different language.

Today, we have a new wave of mission organizations being founded by Christians in countries such as Brazil, South Korea, Nigeria, and China. There are a large number of Indian mission organizations, but their focus is limited to their own country or the Indian diaspora in the Persian Gulf states. Unfortunately, the new breed of evangelists from the countries listed above are generally poorly equipped to evangelize Europe or North America. They know little of Western history and its cultural and intellectual traditions. They repeat all the mistakes of the worst American and British missionaries of earlier times. They get quickly disillusioned and retreat into evangelizing their own ethnic communities.

While migrant/diasporic churches tend to focus, at least initially, on helping their members adjust and cope with day-to-day problems in a majority society that tends to be hostile to newcomers, they retain connections with the local churches they have left behind. Where this becomes problematic is when wealthy migrant pastors in the US, Western Europe, or the Persian Gulf start controlling these churches, through Zoom preaching and sending church-planting teams back home without any consideration for the wider Christian community in that town or village. This is where some of the missiological discussion about the benefits of newer migrant

19. Stanley, *Christianity in the Twentieth Century*, 359.

20. Stanley, *Christianity in the Twentieth Century*, 356.

churches can assume an air of romanticism. The human tendency to empire-building is not confined to white people.

Just like the movement known as "Messianic Jews," the *Christ bhaktars* ("devotees of Christ") and *Isa imandars* ("those faithful to Jesus") of the Indian subcontinent are already, to some degree, practicing the hermeneutics of religious translation: how do we follow Jesus while remaining within our ancestral religious communities, practicing cultural faithfulness, and avoiding unnecessary alienation? The voices of such folk, as well as others who have made a more decisive social break with their traditional religious communities, and identified themselves openly with the visible Christian church, are rarely heard in the ecumenical dialogue fostered by older Christian denominations.

However, there are serious questions to be asked of such "insider movements." One can empathize with those new believers who wish to keep their faith in Christ a secret when the danger of assassination or exclusion is huge. But, as a missiological principle, it can be deceptive and unsustainable. Would we like to see Islamic "insider movements" within the church in Christian-majority countries? Moreover, how can one claim to "follow Jesus" and remain a tribalist? Will not loving one's enemies, as Jesus taught, inevitably involve conflict with our kith and kin? My Israeli Arab, as well as Palestinian Arab, Christian friends tell me how deeply betrayed they feel by the Messianic Jews in Israel who refuse to confront the Israeli apartheid state, and the violence inflicted on Christians and Muslims alike by ultra-orthodox settlers. It seems that Messianic Jews, in their desire to be accepted by fellow Jews, have alienated themselves not only from their Arab Christian brethren, but also from those courageous Jewish scholars and human rights activists who denounce the cruelty of the Zionist state of Israel.

Similarly, it troubles me that *Isa imandars* in Bangladesh seem more than willing to do Bible studies with American and Australian missionaries, but not with the local disciples of Jesus who come from Hindu or tribal backgrounds. I cannot help but wonder: Are other motives involved here? And are these movements replicating the individualistic understandings of the gospel that we have inherited from our colonial forebears and that continue to dominate mission agencies?

We have been reminded in recent decades that all theology is mission theology—that the church does theology "on the road" and not just in the library or the pulpit. But then theological education has to be re-oriented radically around the lives and concerns of "lay" people, not the agendas of clergy and cross-cultural mission agencies. Social and political ethics have become the locus of Evangelical proclamation. And, in societies largely cynical of religious professionals and traditional religion, we need a new generation of thoughtful Christian dramatists, filmmakers, artists, and novelists who know how to indirectly communicate the gospel in ways that grip and transform imaginations, collective and individual. As Pope Benedict XVI once remarked, "The only really effective apologia for Christianity comes down to two arguments, the saints that the church has produced and the art which has grown in her womb.'"[21]

Recovering Our Credibility

The eminent Canadian philosopher Charles Taylor calls the secular age "schizophrenic, or better, deeply cross-pressured."[22] "People," he notes, "seem at a safe distance from religion; and yet they are very moved to know that there are dedicated believers, like Mother Teresa. The unbelieving world, well used to disliking Pius XII, was bowled over by John XXIII. A Pope just had to sound like a Christian, and many immemorial resistances melted."[23]

Whether Roman Catholic, Protestant, Pentecostal, Eastern Orthodox, or whatever, all Christian public witness today has to be *ecumenical* in nature. The days of mono-denominational, mono-ethnic, mono-directional mission are over. Mission is not about expanding my church or denomination but about bearing witness, in word and action, to the Reign of God that is welcomed by weak, sinful, and sinned-against people.

By "ecumenical," I mean the unity of the household of faith that professes the crucified Jesus as the risen Lord of history and the cosmos. The Scriptures make it utterly clear that the credibility of that claim before a cynical world depends crucially on the visible unity of that household. The gospel of reconciliation has to be seen as well as heard. "By this everyone will know that you are my disciples," said our Lord, "if you have love for one another" (John 13:35; also, John 17:20–23). To play off "truth" against "unity" is profoundly misguided. Since truth is relational and

21. Benedict XVI, *Ratzinger Report*, 129–30.

22. Taylor, *Secular Age*, 727.

23. Taylor, *Secular Age*, 727.

eschatological, it can only be discovered, explored, and articulated in the context of a unity-in-diversity.

Perhaps the most depressing statistic in the *Atlas of Global Christianity* is that Christians are more divided than ever.[24] There are more than forty thousand denominations, expected to rise to over fifty-five thousand by 2025.[25] The Korean theologian Moonjang Lee sums up this sorry state of the global church: "Christianity has become too fragmented. Existing in a fragmented world, churches fail to show a united front. There are so many divisions within Christianity that it is an intriguing task to clarify a Christian identity. At the beginning of Christian history, the designation of a person as 'Christian' was sufficient to tell about his or her social, religious, and cultural identity. Today, however, we have to supply subcategories to tell about who we are as Christians, for there are many different and conflicting forms of church life."[26]

The church's ministry of reconciliation, however, if it is to carry credibility among the world's poor and the adherents of non-Christian religious traditions, must begin at home. It must begin by confessing that our fragmentations, divisiveness, and competitive rivalries are a scandal and an affront to the name of Christ.

Churches in the poorer global South are, as we have seen, deeply divided among themselves, but these divisions are accentuated by foreign interventions in the name of "global mission." We are at the receiving end of various initiatives from the rich churches of the North and richer nations of the South (such as Singapore and South Korea). There is little we can do to stop the deluge of obnoxious televangelists, Christian Zionism, the male chauvinist "The Gospel Coalition"[27] and "City to City" courses,[28] so-called "short-term mission trips," and so on. Then there are the sociologically dubious "people-group" methodologies, and the theologically dubious language of "unreached peoples."[29] Popular American preachers and writers are better known in Asia than most Asian Christian scholars. Even church music continues to be imported and translated in many urban churches in

24. Johnson and Ross, *Atlas of Global Christianity*.

25. Johnson and Ross, "Atlas: Its Findings," 193.

26. Lee, "Future of Global Christianity," 104.

27. To find more information, see their website: thegospelcoalition.org.

28. To find more information, see their website: citytocityna.com.

29. For a critique on the concepts of "people groups" and "unreached people groups," see Lee, "Beyond People Group Thinking."

the South. Given the dominance of US material resources on world mission, these trends will continue well into the twenty-first century, even as the majority of long-term, cross-cultural missionaries will be non-Western.

The gospel highlights our human propensity for conflict and divisiveness, as well as acknowledges our deep-seated desire for significant relationships with others. Human beings are not stationary but move across, as well as through, landscapes. Christians bring to public conversations a theological notion of being *pilgrims* as well as citizens. To be a pilgrim is very different from being a mere tourist or proclaiming one's cosmopolitanism in the manner of globalizing elites. There is a moral purpose behind the realization of identity through pilgrimage that is also different from the flight of the refugee or the mere drifter.

As pilgrims, we pay close and prayerful attention to the places and times we inhabit; we remember the narratives and actions that have formed such places and times; we lament and we celebrate, but never seek to possess; and we allow the full symbolic repertoire of the Scriptures to open our imaginations to a world beyond our limited horizons that beckons us forward. Also, Christian pilgrimage, as depicted by Chaucer's *Canterbury Tales*, brings together disparate people who are welded into a community through the exchange of stories with each other and the common sharing of the rigors and hardships of the journey.

Christian unity does not, of course, entail agreement, let alone homogeneity. Christian churches are, after all, bodies of thought and practice which have been formed through diverse histories and social-cultural interactions that cannot be simply ignored. Unity is rather about how we handle our deep-seated disagreements—namely, the way of love: refusing to misrepresent or manipulate others or physically distance ourselves from them. "To remain in communion is to remain in solidarity with those who I believe are wounded as well as wounding the church, in the trust that in the Body of Christ the confronting of wounds is part of opening ourselves to healing."[30]

Tragically, many Christians still allow the secular liturgies of their nation-state (the singing of national anthems, learning narrowly nationalist histories, joining nationalist parades, etc.) to form them into citizens of nations to which they give their fundamental allegiance—even surrendering their bodies uncritically in their defense. Much of the credibility of Christianity in the present millennium will depend on whether we, as

30. Williams, "Making Moral Decisions," 11.

Christians (wherever we happen to live), can resist the deforming identities imposed on us by our nation-state or our ethnic communities, and grasp that our primary identity and allegiance is to Jesus Christ and his universal reign. This is a special challenge today when fragmentation and ideological polarization have come to characterize so much of global politics, and have also infiltrated Christian churches and organizations, and so damaged their witness to Christ.

Finally, the church, while being a distinctive people in the world, is called to show its distinctiveness, not by protecting its borders and separating itself from the world, but by speaking and acting only and always *on behalf of the world.* The church can only defend itself by defending others. In a plural society, Christians secure their religious liberty by advocacy for the liberty of atheists or Jews, Muslims or Hindus: to have the same right to be heard in the continuing conversation about the direction and ethos of a society that is characteristic of a liberal polity. This is a genuine "standing alongside" the "other" in our broken and hurting world; and it is very different from what is called communitarianism, which only links me to people who are like me, and thus, tends to encourage ethnocentric, racist, and even xenophobic tendencies.

"[The church's] credibility does not depend on its unbroken success; only on its continued willingness to be judged by what it announces and points to."[31]

Bibliography

Benedict XVI. *The Ratzinger Report: An Exclusive Interview on the State of the Church.* Interview by Vittorio Messori. Translated by Salvator Attanasio and Graham Harrison. San Francisco: Ignatius, 1985.

Bonhoeffer, Dietrich. *The Cost of Discipleship.* Rev. ed. Translated by Reginald H. Fuller. New York: Macmillan, 1963.

Bosch, David J. *Transforming Mission: Paradigm Shifts in Theology of Mission.* Maryknoll, NY: Orbis, 1991.

Brunner, Emil. *Truth as Encounter: A New Edition, Much Enlarged, of* The Divine-Human Encounter. Translated by Amandus W. Loos and David Cairns. Philadelphia: Westminster, 1964.

Budde, Michael L. *Foolishness to Gentiles: Essays on Empire, Nationalism, and Discipleship.* Eugene, OR: Cascade, 2022.

Chan, Mark. "The Cross Between the Golden Arches and Mickey Mouse." In *Truth to Proclaim: The Gospel in Church and Society*, edited by Simon Chan, 115–36. Singapore: Trinity Theological College, 2002.

31. Williams, "Faith Communities," 306.

Cotterell, Peter. *Mission and Meaninglessness: The Good News in a World of Suffering and Disorder*. London: SPCK, 1990.

Cragg, Kenneth. *The Call of the Minaret*. 2nd ed. London: Collins, 1985.

Ellul, Jacques. *The Subversion of Christianity*. Grand Rapids: Eerdmans, 1986.

Holland, Tom. *Dominion: The Making of the Western World*. London: Little, Brown, 2019.

Ignatius of Antioch. "The Epistle to the Smyrnaeans." In *Early Christian Writings: The Apostolic Fathers*, edited by Andrew Louth, translated by Maxwell Staniforth, 99–105. London: Penguin, 1968.

Johnson, Todd M., and Kenneth R. Ross, eds. *Atlas of Global Christianity*. Edinburgh: Edinburgh University Press, 2009.

———. "The Atlas of Global Christianity: Its Findings." In *Edinburgh 2010: Mission Today and Tomorrow*, edited by Kirsteen Kim and Andrew Anderson, 191–200. Eugene, OR: Wipf & Stock, 2011.

Lee, Moonjang. "Future of Global Christianity." In *Atlas of Global Christianity, 1910–2010*, edited by Todd M. Johnson and Kenneth R. Ross, 104–7. Edinburgh: Edinburgh University Press, 2009.

Lee, Peter T. "Beyond People Group Thinking: A Critical Reevaluation of Unreached People Groups." *Missiology: An International Review* 46 (2018) 212–25.

Maggay, Melba. "The World in Which We Serve: The Impact of Globalization on the Missionary Endeavour of Bible Societies." United Bible Societies. Unpublished manuscript, n.d.

Needham, Joseph. *Within the Four Seas: The Dialogue of East and West*. London: Allen & Unwin, 1964.

O'Donovan, Oliver. *The Desire of the Nations: Rediscovering the Roots of Political Theology*. Cambridge: Cambridge University Press, 1996.

Reisacher, Evelyne. *Joyful Witness in the Muslim World: Sharing the Gospel in Everyday Encounters*. Grand Rapids: Baker Academic, 2016.

Stanley, Brian. *Christianity in the Twentieth Century: A World History*. Princeton: Princeton University Press, 2018.

Taylor, Charles. *A Secular Age*. Cambridge: Harvard University Press, 2007.

Williams, Rowan. "Faith Communities in a Civil Society." Chap. 25 in *Faith in the Public Square*, 302–12. London: Bloomsbury, 2012.

———. "Making Moral Decisions." In *The Cambridge Companion to Christian Ethics*, edited by Robin Gill, 3–15. Cambridge: Cambridge University Press, 2001.

Chapter 4

Tom Skinner and Black Power Evangelicalism

Jemar Tisby

The twelve thousand college students at Urbana '70, the triennial conference on evangelism hosted by the InterVarsity campus ministry, could not have predicted they were about to hear a historic address. Of course, there was still plenty of anticipation for that night's speaker. Tom Skinner, the nationally known Black preacher from Harlem, had already ignited tens of thousands of people with his preaching at evangelistic crusades. What they heard that night was no different.

"Any understanding of world evangelism and racism in our country," Skinner began, "must begin with an understanding of the history of racism."[1] He then traced America's racist history from 1619, when Europeans first brought enslaved Africans to the shores of colonial Virginia up to the late twentieth century. Skinner especially decried the failure of White Christians to address the spiritual and physical well-being of inner-city inhabitants, the masses of Black Americans still struggling to find employment, and those trying to escape the confines of residential segregation.

He reserved his most strident jeremiad for White Christians who, in his view, taught only a Eurocentric version of Jesus. Even though Black residents comprised the vast majority of Harlem, growing up there in the 1950s and 1960s, "all the pictures of Christ were pictures of an Anglo-Saxon,

1. Skinner, "U.S. Racial Crisis," 2:31.

middle-class, Protestant Republican," Skinner said. "There is no way that I can relate to that kind of Christ."[2]

Skinner then made a rhetorical move that his largely White Evangelical audience may not have anticipated. He started talking about systems, revolution, and liberation. "I am a militant; make no bones about it," he proclaimed. "Jesus was militant. And there are those of us who will be called to adopt the militant lifestyle." Skinner soon added an Evangelical inflection to his liberationist discourse. Ending with a fervent charge to evangelize the masses, Skinner shouted, "Proclaim liberation to the captives, preach sight to the blind, set at liberty them that are bruised, go into the world and tell men who are bound mentally, spiritually, and physically, 'The liberator has come!'"[3]

Throughout his ministry, and most explicitly in his speech at Urbana '70, Tom Skinner criticized the failure of White Evangelicals to understand and contextualize the Christian gospel of liberation for oppressed Black people in the United States. His analysis serves as an implicit criticism of international Evangelical missions initiatives, as well. This paper studies the rhetoric of Skinner's speech at Urbana, which was titled "The U.S. Racial Crisis and World Evangelism." If White Evangelicals could not effectively evangelize Black people within their own borders, they would not be able to effectively spread the gospel to Black and Brown peoples globally. More than mere ineffectiveness, however, White Evangelical missions exported a whitewashed Jesus that replicated White cultural norms and proclivities at the expense of indigenous traditions and distinctiveness.

I term Skinner's brand of Christianity "Black Power Evangelicalism" for the ways he incorporated the priorities and principles of the Black Power movement into an Evangelical religious framework. Skinner delivered his speech at Urbana in the midst of the Black Power movement, or what many often called the "Black revolution." Skinner called Jesus the ultimate revolutionary, because the spiritual revolution Jesus promoted went far beyond even what the Black revolutionaries of his day called for in society and politics.

Skinner's speech weaves together familiar Evangelical Christian themes, such as the need for salvation and a personal relationship with Jesus Christ, with elements of Black Power, such as a critique of systemic racial inequality and the call for Black self-sufficiency. While he accepted

2. Skinner, "U.S. Racial Crisis."

3. Skinner, "U.S. Racial Crisis."

Black Power's diagnosis of the racial crisis, he insisted that the "real" revolution consisted in conversion to Christianity and a personal relationship with Jesus Christ. From the blend of these two concepts emerged Black Power Evangelicalism.

Black Power Evangelicalism represented Skinner's synthesis of the racial and political ideas of Black Power with the Christian religious framework presented in Evangelicalism. His upbringing in Harlem steeped him in the thinking of Black nationalists. He had long been familiar with ideas of Black empowerment and the effort to build Black institutions that did not rely on the largesse or whims of White people. After his conversion to Christianity, Skinner's Evangelical beliefs put him in frequent contact with White Evangelical individuals and institutions. Thus, Skinner's discourse reflected attention to both a Black nationalist and a White Evangelical audience.

Tom Skinner's Journey to Evangelicalism

During his lifetime, Tom Skinner became a Black Evangelical leader in thought and ministry, but that trajectory was far from predictable given his early years. For a time during his teenage years, Skinner had lived a double life as the son of a preacher and high-achieving student, as well as a member of a local gang, the Harlem Lords. According to his own claims, he lived a violent life: "By the time I left the gang, I had twenty-two notches on the handle of my knife, which meant that my blade had gone into twenty-two different fellows."[4] All that literally changed overnight after he heard a radio preacher give an invitation to the Christian life. Skinner, who had heard the Christian message of salvation countless times, was finally convinced of it and dedicated his life to sharing this good news.

The next night, Skinner walked into a room filled with his fellow gang members who eagerly awaited their leader's plan of attack. Urban fighters like these men took loyalty seriously, and any defection guaranteed violent retribution. "No one quits a gang. In fact, just two weeks before, I had personally broken the arms and legs of two fellows who told me they were going to quit."[5] Skinner, however, had determined that if his new belief meant anything, then he could not, in good conscience, continue to lead a gang. He stood in front of over one hundred armed gangsters and told them

4. Skinner, *Black and Free*, 56.
5. Skinner, *Black and Free*, 87.

that he had dedicated his life to Christ, so he could no longer lead the Harlem Lords. Although he was prepared to be murdered that night, Skinner walked out of the room "without one person raising a hand" against him.[6] Skinner's conversion story became a key component in his evangelist messages for the rest of his life.

Skinner conducted evangelistic crusades in Harlem and other majority-Black communities. He earned the nickname "The Billy Graham of Harlem."[7] This moniker summarizes the tenor of Skinner's early work as an evangelist in the impoverished, segregated parts of large US cities.

By the time he died in 1994, Skinner had started a Christian nonprofit, held an evangelistic crusade at the historic Apollo Theater in Harlem, became chaplain to the Washington Redskins, and worked as a leadership consultant to major corporations, such as IBM. His funeral had to take place over two different services to accommodate the throngs of people who came to mourn.[8]

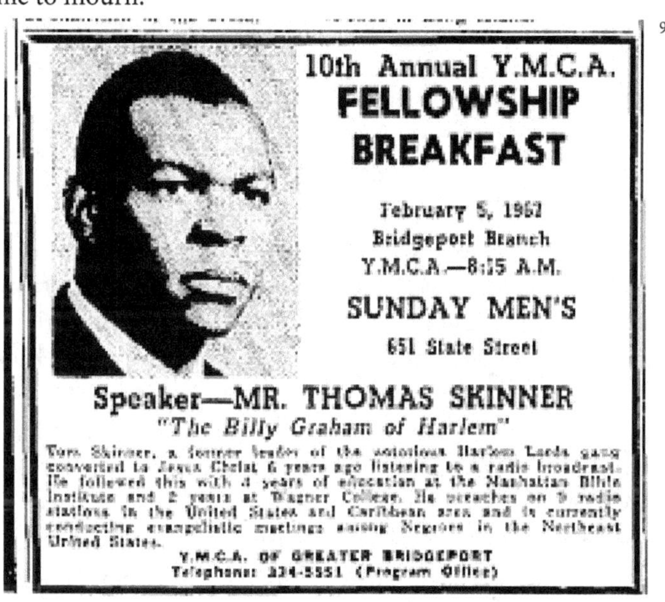

[9]

6. Skinner, *Black and Free*, 87.

7. Y.M.C.A. advertisement. *The Bridgeport Post*, February 4, 1967. Clippings, 1968–1979, Folder 4, Box: 1, Folder: 4. Tom Skinner Papers, CN-430. Evangelism and Missions Archives, Wheaton, IL.

8. Williams-Skinner, *I Prayed, Now What?*, loc. 518.

9. Y.M.C.A. advertisement. *The Bridgeport Post*, February 4, 1967.

Black Power Evangelicalism Confronts White Evangelicalism at Urbana '70

In 1966, Carl Ellis, a Black student at Hampton Institute (now University), attended a leadership training camp hosted by InterVarsity. During the training, a White Evangelical theologian and author, named Clark Pinnock, took an interest in Ellis and said he must meet Tom Skinner. At that point Ellis had never heard of Skinner, but after the camp, another InterVarsity staff member connected the two Black Evangelicals. As a member of the Urbana advisory committee, Ellis remembered his interactions with Skinner and recommended him as a speaker for Urbana '70. The planners agreed, and the stage was set for Skinner's historic address.

The presence of the well-known Black evangelist was just one part of the mission. Now that they had their voice on the stage, they had to get Black students to come to the conference as a larger recruiting strategy. Persuading large numbers of Black college students to attend the majority-White Urbana conference would require directly addressing the issues of racial inequality and the negative perceptions many Black students had about White Evangelicalism.

Ellis helped produce a video called "What Went Down at Urbana '67?" Organizers intended to use the video for promotional purposes. Campus representatives of InterVarsity planned events to show the twenty-one-minute video to groups of college students and then hold a discussion with participants after the viewing. The video, produced in early 1970 and written and directed by Elward Ellis, consciously drew upon Black Power cultural aesthetics and concepts of racial self-awareness.

Various elements of the video—Carl Ellis wearing a dashiki, the funk sounds of the Soul Liberation band during the credits, the all-Black cast, the topics addressed—indicate an engagement with the Black Power movement. The students in the InterVarsity promotional video wanted viewers to know that going to Urbana did not mean they were assimilating to White cultural norms or forgetting the Black struggle for equality. Instead, these young believers attempted to cast a vision of Evangelicalism that fused elements of Black Power with their desire to share the Bible's message with people around the globe.

By this time, Skinner had formed his own organization—"Tom Skinner Associates" (TSA). William "Bill" Pannell, one of Skinner's chief lieutenants in TSA, acquired its manifesto through a friend and decided that the document's ideas had to be folded into the evangelistic message of the organization. Three themes caught Pannell's attention: identity, community, and power. "I sent them to Tom, and we began to work with it. That was the genesis of some thinking about our understanding of the gospel, our understanding of how we are to address the black community."[10] By the time Urbana '70 came, Skinner had incorporated many of the ideas from the Black Power manifesto into his speeches.

Skinner titled his speech at Urbana '70 "The U.S. Racial Crisis and World Evangelism."[11] It represents the evangelist's most concise and impassioned proclamation of Black Power Evangelicalism. In this address, he fuses the discourse and rhetoric of Black Power with the Christian mission of worldwide evangelism. From the start, he focuses on the domestic sphere of evangelism rather than its international dimensions and invites his listeners to ponder the racism of their own communities and country instead of emphasizing the needs of far-off nations. He frames race relations in the United States as a "crisis" that must be addressed if the Christian gospel would advance in Black communities. Skinner urges his listeners to reject a type of religion that viewed social justice and conversion as mutually exclusive. In this moment, Skinner personified the type of religion that many of the Black students wanted to see on display at Urbana, and challenged White Evangelicals to contend with the history of racial inequality in the United States.

An examination of the past undergirds much of Skinner's discourse at Urbana '70. He uses a historical survey of Black experiences in the United States to support his assertion that the nation and the US church was in the midst of a racial crisis. Skinner traces this racial crisis to the nation's past: "To come to grips with what the black revolution is all about . . . I must take you back approximately 350 years to when the early ships landed in this country in approximately 1619."[12] He uses this history to prompt a reevaluation of American exceptionalism. America was not, as Skinner explained, founded as an idyllic democratic experiment by godly Christians who sought to create a just society based on their religious convictions. Rather it had enslavement and injustice at its foundation.

10. William Pannell, phone interview with the author, November 8, 2017. Transcript available upon request.

11. See Skinner's address at Urbana '70: "U.S. Racial Crisis."

12. Skinner, "U.S. Racial Crisis."

In addition to political and economic factors, Skinner also included the "religious system" as a complicit partner in the exploitation of Africans in America. "Numerous churches and denominations preached that slavery was a divine institution ordained by God."[13] He described the so-called "curse of Ham" doctrine. Genesis 9 describes an incident in which one of Noah's sons, Ham, dishonored his father by seeing him naked in a tent after Noah had passed out from too much wine. When Noah awoke, he pronounced a curse: "Cursed be Canaan. The lowest of slaves will he be to his brothers" (Gen 9:25).[14] According to Skinner, "A group of ad hoc dispensationalists argue that Canaan was a descendant of Ham. The word Ham means black; therefore, God has cursed all Black people and relegated them to conditions of servitude."[15] Skinner used this doctrine to point out how enslavers, many of whom claimed to be Christians, justified trafficking in other human beings. These religious people cooperated with a system of economic exploitation, inequality, and violence; and did so in the name of their faith.

Skinner's critique of White Evangelical Christianity centered on their lack of concern for Black people, especially in the inner city: "To a great extent, the Evangelical church in America supported the status quo. . . . It preached against any attempt of the Black man to stand on his own two feet."[16] He continued by decrying the absence of White Evangelicals in communities like the one of his Harlem upbringing.

Huddled in their suburban enclaves, White Evangelicals looked at Black communities with a combination of apathy and fear that kept White Evangelicals from proclaiming good news in inner-city Black neighborhoods. Instead, the message about Black uplift and dignity came not from other Christians, who, even though they were White, professed similar beliefs as Black Christians; but from Black nationalists such as Malcolm X

13. Skinner, "U.S. Racial Crisis."

14. All Scripture quotations in this chapter are taken from the New International Version (NIV).

15. Skinner, "U.S. Racial Crisis," 9:19. The Dispensationalists believe that the Bible is divided into different periods, or "dispensations," that describe God's dealings with humankind. A part of dispensationalist belief focuses on the promised return of Jesus Christ. In this tradition, Jesus will only return after a prolonged period of evil and chaos in the world. Thus, many dispensationalists focused on evangelizing non-Christians and seeking their conversion rather than pursuing social, political, and economic justice in a world that was destined to only get worse before Christ returned.

16. Skinner, "U.S. Racial Crisis."

and the Nation of Islam. Such a blunt appraisal of the failings of White Evangelicals in regard to evangelizing and expressing solidarity with Black people was not the norm at an overwhelmingly White Christian event, such as Urbana '70.

In the second half of his speech, Skinner turned his attention to evangelism. After detailing his own conversion from a gang leader to a Christian evangelist, he explained his concept of "revolution." Malcolm X's concept of revolution orbited around the acquisition of land. He called land the basis of "freedom, justice, and equality."[17] In pursuit of land, Black revolutionaries had to be willing to use force. "Revolution is bloody, revolution is hostile, revolution knows no compromise, revolution overturns and destroys everything that gets in its way."[18] Malcolm X espoused the philosophy of Black liberation "by any means necessary," a stance which proved unacceptable to many Black Christians, such as Skinner.

Skinner redefined "revolution" within the context of Black Power Evangelicalism. "First, the definition of a revolution is to take an existing situation, which has proved to be unworkable, archaic, impractical, and out of date; you seek to destroy it, and overthrow it, and replace it with a system that works," he explained.[19] According to this definition, Skinner declared that Jesus Christ was a revolutionary. Christ came "to overthrow the demonic human system and establish his own kingdom in the hearts of men."[20] In contrast to Malcolm X's assertion that revolution meant a possibly violent conflict in order to secure physical land, Skinner recasts revolution as a fundamentally spiritual event that takes place in the heart. The system that needs to be overthrown, according to Black Power Evangelicalism, is primarily the inclination to sin and transgress against God.

Black Power Evangelicalism attempted to lift the gaze of its adherents from an earthly revolution to a spiritual one. The leader of the revolution Skinner talked about was not Malcolm X, Stokely Carmichael, Angela Davis, or any other well-known figure of the Black Power movement, but Jesus Christ himself. Unlike White Evangelicalism, Skinner's Black Power Evangelicalism did not wave away issues of racial injustice by assuming that change would automatically happen after enough people converted to Christianity. Instead, Black Power Evangelicals, such as Skinner, recognized

17. Malcolm X, "Message to the Grassroots," 266.

18. Malcolm X, "Message to the Grassroots," 266.

19. Skinner, "U.S. Racial Crisis."

20. Skinner, "U.S. Racial Crisis."

the material concerns of Black people and insisted that comprehensive change had to occur at both the social and the spiritual level. Skinner's vision of Evangelicalism indicted Black Power activists who neglected the inner spiritual revolution he believed had to take place. He also condemned White Evangelical fantasies that a profession of religion would eliminate material poverty and racial inequality.[21]

In order to spread the gospel of Black Power Evangelicalism, Christians had to go out and proclaim liberation to all kinds of oppressed people. Skinner commissioned his listeners to become "infiltrators," who acted as agents of revolution in every arena of society.[22] While some Christians formed their own colleges and universities, book publishing companies, and fellowships in order to avoid "worldliness," Skinner presented a vision of missionary activity that entailed going into non-Christian spaces in order to represent Jesus Christ, the revolutionary.[23] The mission called for Christians to be as bold and uncompromising as any revolutionary army, with one crucial difference: "But keep in mind that militancy and radicalism must be disciplined and controlled by the Word of God and by the Holy Spirit."[24]

Black Power Evangelicalism challenged Christians not to reject the rhetoric of revolution, but to reframe it in religious terms. Just as leaders in the Black Power movement were calling their followers to mission and sacrifice for the sake of overturning corrupt systems of power and money, Black Power Evangelicals called their followers to be part of a "new order" and stage a coup against the works of the Devil. Thus, Skinner did not advocate for armed conflict. He did not promote physical violence as a means to racially just ends. Rather, his teachings hewed closely to the Bible verse that says, "For though we live in the world, we do not wage war as the world does. The weapons we fight with are not the weapons of the world. On the contrary, they have divine power to demolish strongholds" (2 Cor 10:3–4).

Apparently, Skinner's Black power version of Evangelicalism resonated with students. Bill Pannell recalled, "When he finished that thing, the whole audience exploded. I'd never seen a response like that anywhere.

21. Skinner, "U.S. Racial Crisis."

22. Skinner, "U.S. Racial Crisis," 44:04.

23. For more on the growth of separate Christian institutions, see works such as Laats, *Fundamentalist U*; Gloege, *Guaranteed Pure*; Miller, *Age of Evangelicalism*; Marsden, *Reforming Fundamentalism*; and Williams, *God's Own Party*.

24. Skinner, "U.S. Racial Crisis."

It was almost as if all of the seats had been wired, and someone pressed a button, and all the electricity ran through those seats, and everyone jumped in the air. . . . It was astonishing."[25] Even the White students responded with excitement. "The Whites were blown away too; they just thought it was a powerful speech," remembered Carl Ellis, Jr.[26] In an interview four months after his speech, Skinner himself offered this reflection: "Urbana was the most significant missionary conference in the last decade."[27] Although Skinner's speech came on the second day of the five-day conference, it remained the high point of the entire week for many.

Not everyone received Skinner's message at Urbana '70 so positively. Just over a week after the conference ended, Warren B. Appleton, the White father of a student who attended Urbana, typed an angry letter to John Alexander, the president of InterVarsity.[28] He objected to Skinner's appropriation of the words "revolution" and "revolutionaries," which Appleton associated with Communism. "The net results are that twelve-thousand of America's finest young, idealist[ic], Christian intellectuals are mis-lead into giving a standing ovation to a speaker demanding overthrow of the present order he branded as Satanic, while the musicians brandished Communist clenched-fist salutes."[29] Appleton ended with a challenge to Alexander and the other leaders of InterVarsity to explain why they would permit such messages to be part of Urbana.[30]

Skinner continued to speak in the language of Black Power Evangelicalism, and as he did, others became agitated. In April of 1971, the Moody Bible Institute radio station, WMBI, cancelled Skinner's thirty-minute weekly program, because "the broadcast has been becoming increasingly

25. William Pannell, interview by Robert Shuster, June 1990, transcript, tape 7. William E. Pannell Oral History Interviews, CN 498. Evangelism and Missions Archives, Wheaton, IL.

26. Carl F. Ellis Jr., telephone interview with author, October 15, 2017. Transcript available upon request.

27. "Interview with Tom Skinner," Urbana &, Vol. 1, No. 6, April 1, 1971. Clippings, 1968–1979, Folder 4, Box: 1, Folder: 4. Tom Skinner Papers, CN-430. Evangelism and Missions Archives, Wheaton, IL.

28. Warren B. Appleton, letter to John Alexander, January 9, 1971. Billy Graham Center Archives, Call Number 300, Records of the President, John Alexander: Correspondence, Box 38, Folder 11, Wheaton, IL.

29. Appleton, letter to John Alexander.

30. Appleton, letter to John Alexander.

political, with less emphasis on God's message to all men."[31] The managers of the station had become concerned that Skinner's insistence on discussing issues of racism and injustice would alienate their White Evangelical listeners.[32]

These responses indicated that a message challenging the social and political outlook of White Evangelicals could be the source of controversy. White Evangelicals favorably received Skinner as an evangelist who talked about soul winning, but not as a Christian who taught a race-conscious and socially active faith. Although subsequent correspondence shows Skinner stayed in touch with the White leaders of InterVarsity, he never spoke at an Urbana conference again.

After arriving home from another speaking engagement in the spring of 1994, Tom Skinner's wife picked him up from the airport. She could immediately tell that her husband was in agonizing pain, so she called a physician. The diagnosis was leukemia. It took just two and a half months from the time a doctor diagnosed Skinner's acute condition for the disease to claim his life on June 17.[33] The people who came to his funeral attest to his broad and diverse influence. Black Power leaders, including Betty Shabazz, Dick Gregory, and Louis Farrakhan attended, as well as other black dignitaries, such as Jesse Jackson and Maya Angelou. While few would consider Skinner a Black Power activist, his familiarity with the circumstances of Black ghettoes, his ability to fuse Black Power principles with Evangelical Christian beliefs, and his lifelong commitment to forging lasting personal relationships kept him in contact with the racial consciousness movement, even after the height of the Black Power movement in the late 1960s and 1970s.

Conclusion

Skinner's extensive contact with White Evangelicals meant that he had a unique vantage point to understand their racial beliefs, fears, and perspectives. It allowed him and his associates to communicate Black Power in the Evangelical idiom. He could speak eloquently about the need for personal conversion, and at the same time, recast Jesus as a liberatory figure

31. E. Brandt Gustavson, memo from Moody Broadcasting Department, April 14, 1971.

32. Gustavson, memo.

33. Williams-Skinner, *I Prayed, Now What?*, loc. 508.

willing to preach hope and freedom to the Black people of the ghetto that Evangelicals often feared or overlooked. White Evangelicals tended to give Skinner a hearing in a way they afforded to only a select few Black people. Compared to those in historically Black denominations or Christians who took more liberal views of theology and the Bible, Skinner had a chance to influence White Evangelicals as a relative insider.[34]

Yet Skinner's emphasis on a race-conscious Christianity and a Black Power–infused Evangelicalism also posed a threat to White Evangelical myths of colorblindness and racial innocence. The very realities of which Skinner made his audiences aware had the potential to undermine White Evangelical power structures and patterns of ministry. In regard to missions both domestically and internationally, Skinner's Black Power Evangelicalism disrupted ideas of White centrality and Eurocentric versions of Christianity that sought to convert people not only to a religion but to a white way of life. Skinner's race-conscious approach to Christianity inherently threatened an ideology of missions based explicitly on colorblindness and implicitly on the superiority of White theology, culture, and conceptions of Christ.

Bibliography

Gloege, Timothy. *Guaranteed Pure.* Chapel Hill: University of North Carolina Press, 2015.

Laats, Adam. *Fundamentalist U: Keeping the Faith in American Higher Education.* Oxford: Oxford University Press, 2018.

Malcolm X. "A Message to the Grassroots." In *The Portable Malcolm X Reader*, edited by Manning Marable and Garrett Felber, 265–73. New York: Penguin, 2013.

Marsden, George. *Reforming Fundamentalism: Fuller Seminary and the New Evangelicalism.* Grand Rapids: Eerdmans, 1995.

Miller, Steven P. *The Age of Evangelicalism.* New York: Oxford University Press, 2014.

Skinner, Tom. *Black and Free.* Rev. ed. Maitland, FL: Xulon, 2005.

———. "The U.S. Racial Crisis and World Evangelism." Urbana 25, Jan. 29, 2015. YouTube, 58:10. https://www.youtube.com/watch?v=bvKQx4ycTmA.

Williams, Daniel K. *God's Own Party: The Making of the Christian Right.* Oxford: Oxford University Press, 2010.

Williams-Skinner, Barbara. *I Prayed, Now What? My Journey from No Faith to Deep Faith.* Tracy's Landing, MD: Skinner Leadership Institute, 2008. Kindle.

34. For example, Albert Cleage Jr., of the Shrine of the Black Madonna in Detroit, MI, would have been perceived as too radical and militant for mainstream Evangelical outlets. Others, such as Joseph H. Jackson, president of the National Baptist Convention (NBCUSA, Inc.) had views of Scripture and doctrine that closely mirrored that of White Evangelicals, but he inhabited a world of Black churches that did not rely on White Evangelical institutions or approval to exist.

Chapter 5

Dangerous Women and the Promise of Purity

Jessica Wai-Fong Wong

Sex isn't the only taboo for unmarried women, according to the Evangelical church in which my student grew up; the use of tampons and gynecological visits are also on the list of unacceptable behaviors. Penetration of any kind—even by cotton or speculum—is thought to diminish a woman's virginity. While many of us would consider the prohibition of Tampax and visits to an ob-gyn as extreme, the impetus behind these rules is familiar to many within Christian circles.

Purity Culture, which gained popularity in the 1990s, is a Christian Evangelical movement that focuses on promoting abstinence prior to marriage. It pursues this end by teaching young women that every time they engage in sex outside of marriage, they give part of themselves away, functionally diminishing the gift of *self* communicated in any sexual encounter with their future spouse.

Young men tend to be given a different lesson, one that speaks to the importance of guarding against their natural inclination toward the sin of lust, which purportedly courses more strongly within them than it does their biologically female counterparts. They are taught that only by staving off such impure impulses can they remain strong men of faith. While for both parties the goal is sexual abstinence, the underlying message given as to why one should abstain is notably distinct, as is the response to instances of transgression. While this difference might be attributable to a cultural, "boys-will-be-boys-type" attitude, there are nonetheless underlying ecclesial and theological aspects present as well. What are the theological factors that have led to the church's seemingly heightened investment in the embodiment of women? What makes women's bodily functions and conducts of particular interest to the church?

One might raise a similar question about Evangelical attitudes around abortion. According to a Pew Research survey from March 2022, 74 percent of White Evangelicals believe that abortion should be illegal in all or most cases, and are twice as likely as the average American (and more likely than any other religious group) to support abortion bans.[1] Acknowledging the religious roots of their conviction, it is possible that this level of support is the result of a deeply held belief in the sanctity of life, especially the life of a vulnerable child. It is curious, however, that such a conviction does not extend to other areas of life—to child-related social services, the death penalty, or even the availability of guns, which is now the leading cause of child mortality in the United States.[2] The incongruity between such positions creates space to question whether there might be other factors impacting this unique level of concern over abortion.[3]

It is perhaps an unspoken truth that the litmus test for whether one is a true Christian within Evangelical circles can be distilled to three issues: sex, sexuality, and abortion. Now that I've, perhaps unwisely, opened this paper with two of the three, I would like to clarify one thing: The point I'm raising here is not whether there are valid theological arguments for abstinence or against abortion. (Stanley Hauerwas provides a particularly good pro-life argument based on the call of Christian community.[4]) Rather, the question I'm posing is this: Might there be something deeper driving the Evangelical discourse around sexual purity and abortion?

The church has long demonstrated particular interest in the bodies and embodiment of certain people, women being among them. What drives this attentiveness? While the commonly articulated values of purity and life are certainly present in Evangelical Christianity's focus on bodies and embodiment, I suspect that beneath these convictions is a more fundamental concern: that of proper order. The story being told is that God has

1. Shellnutt, "White Evangelicals Twice," para. 5.
2. Soerens, "This Love of Guns"; Villarreal et al., *Gun Violence*, 6.
3. Balmer, "Religious Right."
4. Hauerwas, "Abortion, Theologically Understood (1991)."

established a holy order according to which Christians are to live, and that certain people—including women—pose a threat to this order of things.

Philosophical and Theological Readings of Women

Even before we get to theological writings on the disorderly nature of women, the inherent inferiority of the female sex is already present within Greek philosophy. Rooted in the belief that the woman lacks the active heat necessary to form life, Aristotle concludes that when it comes to the reproductive formation of a child *in utero*, it is the man alone who contributes the soul, or *logos*, that gives shape to the unformed material substance that the woman passively provides. The man is therefore the primary cause or mover in the reproductive process. His active power, "as the proximate motive cause, to which belong the logos and the Form, is better and more divine in its nature than the Matter. . . . That is why wherever possible and so far as possible the male is separate from the female, since it is something better and more divine in that it is the principle of movement for generated things, while the female serves as their matter."[5] Aristotle's assertion that the active power of the male is not only "better" but also "more divine" is rooted in the fact that the divinity of the "first principle" provided by the man is the *logos*. And this *logos* is tied to the rational soul of man as well as the rationality of the divine.

In Aristotle's writing, we find an early instantiation of what will later become a well-established trope concerning men and women—namely, that men are marked by a natural rationality and, in this case, a kind of transcendent reason that is unavailable to women. Women, instead, are characterized by an irrationality tied to their embodiment.[6] They are governed by the baser principles of their emotions and instincts, rooted in women's connection with the material world and their bodies.

These Greek philosophical ideas are not alien to Christian theology, of course. Augustine of Hippo, for example, claims that because God is *Logos* (Reason), it follows that humans bear the image of God through holy contemplation, an activity rooted in the mind-soul. Such contemplative activity is our human reason seeking the Reason that is God, our *logos* seeking the great *Logos*. What is notable about Augustine's conception of the *Imago Dei*,

5. Aristotle, *Generation of Animals*, 732a.3–11.

6. For more on the development of the trope of female irrationality, see Lloyd, "Man of Reason."

however, is that he does not believe that both men and women manifest the image of God to the same degree. Men are more rational than women and, therefore, bear the image of God more thoroughly. He writes,

> The woman together with her own husband is the image of God, so that the whole substance may be one image; but when she is referred separately to her quality of *help-meet*, which regards the woman herself alone, then she is not the image of God; but as regards the man alone, he is the image of God as fully and completely as when the woman too is joined with him in one.[7]

According to this reading of the substantive *Imago Dei*, it is due to men's natural rationality, which stands over-against women's embodied irrationality, that men are able to image God apart from women, but women must be joined with men to image God. Men are simply more aligned with the holy (rational and transcendent) order of God.

By the medieval period, this picture of women as less rational, less transcendent, and therefore less compatible with the divine *oikonomia* that is God's holy order, has had plenty of time to take hold.[8] Stories of women's diminished rationality and materially bound existence has been rehearsed in biological, philosophical, and theological spheres. In the *Summa*, Thomas Aquinas reiterates Aristotle's argument that it is because of the woman's "defective and misbegotten" nature that she contributes nothing formative to the reproductive process.[9] It is the male seed alone that provides the active power necessary to give shape to the unborn child. Given the superior nature of active to passive, "the male seed tends to the production of a perfect likeness in the masculine sex; while the production of a woman comes from defect in the active power."[10] Put simply, when the active power is sufficiently manifest, the baby is born a boy. When the active power is deficient, the baby is born a girl.[11] Now, even if we accept that

7. Augustine, *On the Trinity* 12.7.10 (*NPNF*[1] 3:159).

8. As I note elsewhere, economy (*oikonomia*), as a general term, refers to the proper management, organization, or administration of a household or society that is marked by the goal of securing the well-being of said household or society. Within the Christian context, divine economy refers to "the rhythm that organizes and orders the material and spiritual realms in a manner consistent with God's salvific plan, for it is at least partly within this salvific register that economy secures the well-being of creation." Wong, 29.

9. Aquinas, *Summa theologica* I, q.92, a. 1, ad. 1.

10. Aquinas, *Summa theologica* I, q.92, a. 1, ad. 1.

11. It is notable that this same concept of the female as a "mutilated male" is present in Aristotle's work as well. See Aristotle, *Works of Aristotle*, II.3 (737a.27).

this view of the female sex as deficient is limited to the biological process, we are nonetheless left with the fact that women are thought to lack the necessary active power because they lack sufficient *logos* rationality.[12] It is, after all, the rational soul within men that allows them to exercise the active power that imparts form to the material substance that becomes a child. If the woman lacks this rational *logos*, or manifests it in diminished form, what does this say about her capacity to commune with, or image, God?[13]

Much like Augustine, Aquinas sees the soul as the incorporeal site of human intellect.[14] It both corresponds with the body and is superior to it. This correspondence of soul to body is akin to a kind of reflection. The body reflects the state of the soul. Such a correspondence helps explain Aquinas's belief in female deficiency. He writes, "It is necessary for the soul to be proportioned to the body, as form to matter, and as mover to moved; and therefore woman, even as to her soul, was more imperfect than man."[15] In short, the inferior state of the woman's soul corresponds with the deficiencies of her body, and the deficiencies of her body provide insight into the deficiencies of her soul. The incompletion of the woman is not only physical but also spiritual.

Women's Fallen Legacy

Aquinas's gesture toward the corresponding nature of spirit and body reflects an established sense within medieval thought that spiritual order is not simply an internal condition impacting the moral, intellectual, and emotional realms; it is also manifest externally in the form and function of the body. For women, such logic is used to explain the female menstrual cycle. As daughters of Eve, all women bear the spiritual consequences of the first woman's disobedience. While both Adam and Eve ate of the tree of the knowledge of good and evil, it was Eve who spoke to the serpent, an animal symbolically associated with "bestial and demonic order."[16] It was Eve who first submitted to temptation, eating of the Tree of Knowledge. As 1 Timothy puts it, "Adam was not deceived, but the woman was deceived

12. Nolan, "Aristotelian Background," 59–68.
13. Horowitz, "Aristotle and Woman," 194.
14. Aquinas, *Summa theologica* I, q.75, a. 2.
15. Lohr, *St. Thomas Aquinas*.
16. Resnick, *Marks of Distinction*, 44.

and became a transgressor."[17] According to this reading of Gen 3, Adam's sin is subsequent and secondary to that of Eve's. It is Eve who is the primary cause of the Fall. It is Eve who rejects the proper order that God gifts the humans and, in doing so, submits herself to the serpent's bestial disorder. In this act of disobedience, the woman privileges her material and carnal desires over the rational and spiritual directive of God. She elevates the serpent's instability and falsehood above divine form and truth, thereby choosing for herself a less transcendent, less rational, and more animalistic, materially bound existence.[18]

The ontological deformation that occurs within Eve is then passed down from generation to generation, from mother to daughter, such that all women now bear the consequences of her disobedience. Choosing guttural desire over divine rationality, some medieval texts go so far as to suggest that it is because of Eve that women no longer bear the *Imago Dei* at all. Instead, theirs is the *imago* of a wild beast.[19] It is for this reason that men are judged naturally superior to women in both spirit and mind.[20]

As previously noted, this lapsarian corruption inherited from Eve does more than impact the nature of a woman's intellectual and spiritual state; it alters her physiologically, as well. According to medieval medical thought, the body is ruled by humors; consisting of blood, yellow bile, black bile, and phlegm; which are themselves tied to the elemental qualities of cold, hot, moist, and dry. In order to maintain bodily health, all four humors must be kept in proper balance: they must be rightly ordered. However, the spiritual corruption that the woman inherits from Eve leaves her in a state of perpetual humoral imbalance, resulting in an excessively moist and cold complexion.

The consequence of this imbalance is twofold. First, the woman's inordinately moist and cold complexion leaves her sexually dissatisfied. Her desire burns like damp wood, continuing to smolder in search of gratification. As a result, the medieval Christian woman is believed to be more inclined toward sexual infidelity than the average Christian man.[21]

17. 1 Tim 2:14 NRSVue.

18. William of Auxerre, *Summa Aurea* 2, tr. 9, cap. 1, q. 3; cited in Resnick, *Marks of Distinction*, 51.

19. Resnick, *Marks of Distinction*, 45.

20. Albert the Great, *De incarnatione* tr. 3, q. 2, a. 4; cited in Resnick, *Marks of Distinction*, 52.

21. Resnick, *Marks of Distinction*, 27.

Women are believed to be so prone to sexual sin that when men engage in inappropriate sexual behavior they are said to "turn away from higher things and to become, like a woman, bound to the body."[22] A temptress by nature, Albert the Great describes the woman as a "venomous serpent" and "nothing but a devil fashioned into a human appearance."[23] This connection that Albert makes between women and the serpent of Gen 3 is not altogether uncommon in medieval writings. After all, not only is Eve tempted by the serpent, but she takes on the role of the serpent when she, in turn, lures Adam into disobedience. This explains the medieval paintings of the Fall that portray the serpent with the body of a snake and the head of a woman.[24] Just as Adam should have been wary of Eve, who lured him into disobedience, the Christian man should also exercise caution.

In addition to a tendency toward wayward sexual behavior, the woman's humoral imbalance leads to an accumulation of toxins within her body. This noxious buildup produces both emotional and physical consequences, including that of "mania" and "leprosy."[25] Her body must expel these toxins regularly if she is to avoid such illnesses.[26] Menstruation, then, is a byproduct of the first woman's spiritual corruption and a sign of female fallenness. Menstruation is an indirect consequence of betrayal.

Jews and Heretics

Women, of course, are not the only ones thought to fall victim to the spiritual corruption that attends abandoning God's intended plan in exchange

22. Karras, *Sexuality in Medieval Europe*, 30.

23. Albert the Great, *Questions* 15.11.

24. One finds examples of this in Michelangelo's *The Fall of Man* (also known as *The Fall and Expulsion from the Garden of Eden*), c. 1509–1510, fresco, Sistine Chapel, Vatican City; and Masolino da Panicale's *Temptation of Adam and Eve*, c. 1425–1427, fresco, Brancacci Chapel, Santa Maria del Carmine, Florence.

25. Thomas of Wrocław, *Thomae de Wratislavia Practica medicinalis*, 72; cited in Resnick, *Marks of Distinction*, 178. Also see Mondzain, *Image, Icon, Economy*, 13. For some time, this humor imbalance was thought to cause the uterus to become "restless and migratory," resulting in female hysteria. Tasca et al. "Women and Hysteria." Thus, hysteria was seen as a predominantly female illness, a belief that persists well into the nineteenth century, and even today remains present with us in the trope of the hysterical woman. While the spiritual cause of female hysteria dissipated over time, one must wonder whether there remains an implicit sense of culpability placed upon women for what is perceived to be extreme emotional (over)reactions.

26. Resnick, *Marks of Distinction*, 23.

for a bestial and demonic disorder. Nor, interestingly enough, are they the only ones to suffer the physiological consequences of menstruation. Medieval texts suggest that Jews and heretics are also afflicted by this same external manifestation of internal corruption. As historian Sander Gilman describes the position taken up by thirteenth-century theologian Thomas de Cantimpré, "male Jews menstruated as a mark of the 'Father's curse,' their pathological difference [being] a result of their original denial of Christ."[27]

Fittingly, this bloody punishment that marks the spiritually disordered Jew and heretic parallels the fate of another who has rejected Christ. According to the book of Acts, upon hanging himself, Judas's intestines spill from his body.[28] Commentaries from late antiquity augment this biblical depiction with the claim that, upon his death, his soul exits his body by way of his anus. It is this departure of the soul from the body that constitutes his bloody evacuation.[29] Like both Jew and heretic, Judas's betrayal of God is what triggers his gruesome fate. To reject Christ is to reject God's divine economy, and in doing so, to embrace its opposite. It is to embrace the devil's demonic disorder. For, just as the devil is thought to enter the body by way of the anus, the soul of the deceitful and spiritually corrupt is believed to leave the body likewise. Thus, "anal retribution" is the fate of all who reject or betray God's divine economy.[30]

By claiming that male menstruation is the natural consequence of choosing spiritual disorder over God's divine ways, medieval writers reinforce the narrative of women's inherent disorderliness. For, according to this logic, almost all women bear the physiological marks of this inherent spiritual corruption.

27. Gilman, *Jewish Self-Hatred*, 74–75; cited in Johnson, "Myth of Jewish Male Menses," 273–74.

28. Acts 1:18.

29. The *Glossa Ordinaria* notes that Judas's "bowels . . . which were the seat of deceit, were burst by so great a crime that they were unable to contain themselves. Fittingly, then, through the seat of fraud the bowels were poured out, not through the place of the kiss—the mouth with which Jesus was kissed, though with foul intent—but through another place, by which the poison of hidden malice had entered"; cited in Johnson, "Myth of Jewish Male Menses," 279.

30. Willis Johnson provides an insightful analysis of the reported fate of Arius of Alexandria, suggesting that, according to medieval writers, Arius's heretical betrayal of Jesus leads to this "symbolic scatological death." According to Johnson, this belief reflects a "narrative of oral transgression and anal retribution [that] initiated a motif in Christian writing that evolved centuries later into the myth of the Jewish male menses." Johnson, "Myth of Jewish Male Menses," 278.

Societal Threat

Not only do women suffer the consequences of their own corrupt spiritual state, but their internal disorder is also believed to be contagious. In fact, medieval medical texts advise Christian men to avoid sexual contact with women during menses, lest they be tainted by female fallenness. If intercourse does occur, the toxicity of the woman's menstrual blood risks contaminating the man's proper spiritual order, thereby altering his own humoral balance and resulting in bodily sickness, such as leprosy.[31] Men should take care when engaging women in a state of impurity. The same dangers of physical exposure apply to children born to menstruating mothers. It is believed that a newborn can contract a congenital disease through contact with menses at the time of their birth.[32]

While this science may now strike us as suspect on a number of levels, the lesson being communicated at the time was clear: a person's internal state is manifest externally.[33] And one can see this clearly in the case of women, for all women have inherited the spiritual corruption of Eve's rejection of God's good order, and embrace of its opposite. Women now bear the consequences of this spiritual affliction not only in their mental, moral,

31. Resnick, *Marks of Distinction*, 118. St. Bonaventure claims that the "unclean thoughts, disordered desires, and wicked and deceitful images of women" produce "corrupt humors and disordered desires in the flesh," including "scabies . . . and sometimes leprosy, which remove the cleanness of the body" (Bonaventure, *Sermones dominicales*, *Sermo* 43.8.134).

32. The idea that conception during menstruation produces monstrous children can be traced as far back as the Greco-Roman period and persists well into the Middle Ages. The apocryphal 2 Esdras, for example, provides an account of the Hebrew scribes' encounter with an angel who spoke to him about the coming signs of the end times, when "menstruous women shall bring forth monsters" (2 Esd 5:8).

33. This concept of the external manifestation of one's internal state allows for the inverse association—assessment of the external attributes of the body as a way of gaining insight into the truth of one's internal spiritual, moral, emotional, intellectual, and sociopolitical character. It is in accordance with this belief that we get medieval stories of Jewish men who convert to Christianity, and, upon their baptism, experience what art historian and medieval scholar Pamela Patton calls a "miraculous rhinoplasty," essentially changing the shape of the Jewish nose. Merback, ed. *Beyond the Yellow Badge*, 239. Extending beyond the Middle Ages, this way of thinking is also present in pseudosciences like nineteenth-century phrenology and physiognomy, as well as in the Victorian argument against women's civic participation. In this latter case, it is the frailty of women's bodies that acts as an indication of their enfeebled intellects and emotional predispositions, rendering them ill-suited for political participation. See Mosedale, "Science Corrupted."

and emotional states, but also in their physical bodies. Whether by way of leprosy or monthly period, the body reveals the truth of the woman's waywardness. What's more, her inherent corruption is contagious. Others can be infected through contact with the physical manifestations of her disorder.

The Body Politic

This last claim concerning the infectious nature of the woman's corruption is sociopolitically significant. For, within the context of Christendom, a society organized around what is perceived to be the holy order of God, good citizenship is determined by the extent to which one lives in accordance with this divine economy. It follows that those believed to manifest a dissonant order are also thought to pose a real threat to the function and future of Christian society. This is particularly pronounced in the case of women, who are thought to easily pass their disorder on to others. Threatening the proper order of others in this way, women endanger the whole of civilized Christian society.

Of course, this assessment of risk is not limited to women; it applies to non-Christians and heretics as well. They, too, embody the same type of spiritual disorder that threatens Christendom's health and flourishing. The difference, however, is that, while it is possible during the Middle Ages to remove Jews, Moors, and heretics from the body politic through edicts of expulsion, inquisition, and exile; the solution is not so simple when it comes to Christian women. As bearers of Christian boys who will one day become faithful men and good citizens, women are indispensable. The solution, when it comes to Christian women, cannot be expulsion or extermination. Instead, female waywardness must be reformed. Women of faith must be encouraged to cultivate control over their bodily bound corruption and disorderliness, so as to bring themselves into greater alignment with God's proper order. And men of faith must provide the guidance to aid them in this endeavor.

Virginal Aspirations

Despite women's natural state of corruption, medieval thinkers, nonetheless, recognize that biology is not destiny. Even for Aquinas, with his views of female inferiority, there are exceptions to the rule. It is possible for a woman to transcend her bestial corruption so as to attain a higher state of existence. We see examples of this transcendence in hagiographies of female saints, wherein they prove that they are not "bound to the body," but are spiritually pure. Physical virginity is, of course, one way of indicating such purity. But it is perhaps even more profoundly displayed in their transcendence of the "common nature" of the flesh, as one observes in certain patristic hagiographies.[34] One finds a similar theme of bodily transformation in the stories of the female saints from the Middle Ages, as well. More frequently than their male counterparts, these holy women appear to undertake spiritual practices focused on taming the body's physical needs. They are also more likely to experience the gift of stigmata, as their own bodies are brought into conformity with that of our crucified Lord.[35]

This, of course, is a spiritual avenue available to the female saints. But what of the typical Christian woman, one who has not taken monastic vows, but nonetheless desires to live faithfully? What kind of path to purity is available to her? After all, it is the purity of the laywoman that is of greatest consequence to Christian society, for not only do such women have the ability to corrupt Christian men, but their reproductive role is essential to its future.

Christian society's anxious preoccupation over women's purity is manifest in the reoccurring medieval motif of the non-Christian man, who threatens the sexual and spiritual virtue of the faithful woman.[36] It can also be observed in the cautionary tale of the woman who, at the moment of inception, allows herself to imagine a grotesque, bestial, or dark image, and as a result, bears a disfigured child.[37] While these stories are clearly different, they nonetheless point to a shared idea—failure to protect female purity can have dangerous reproductive consequences. More than a lust for control and power, the driving sentiment is that of fear, namely fear

34. Gregory of Nyssa, *Ascetical Works*, 179.

35. Coakley, "Powers of Holy Women," 10.

36. Howard, "Female Saints," 76.

37. It is interesting to note that various versions of this story describe the dark image differently. While some accounts speak of the image as that of a demon or dwarf, others claim it to be an Ethiopian. The principle in all of these accounts, however, is the same. As Thomas of Cantimpré notes in his writings on the natural world, "The nature of the woman is such, that whatever they look upon or think about at the moment of conception will affect the appearance of the child. For an animal, while mating, transmits inwardly the form of the things seen outside and, when filled with the images, takes their forms into their own substance" (Thomas of Cantimpré, *De natura rerum* [Lib. 55–12], 253, fol. 4r in Resnick, *Marks of Distinction*, 298).

of societal disorder fueled by the desire to preserve what is believed to be God's intentions for society.[38]

While it is easy to interpret Christianity's history of control over women's bodies as simply a product of patriarchal grasping (and this very well may be part of the story), a more textured reading suggests that the rules and regulations applied to female embodiment is also the by-product of a desire to be faithful. The demands for purity applied to young girls, and even the punitive approaches to regulating women's bodies, come, at least in part, from a place of conviction and best intentions, perhaps even from the desire for all people to know the blessings of a life properly ordered before God.

A Question of Divine Order

But herein lies the real question: What if the order we believe to be "of God" is more a reflection of our own human culture than the divine reality? Scripture is replete with examples of people believing themselves to be living according to the order of God and being taught otherwise. We see this in Peter's vision of the blanket of unclean food, and his subsequent meeting with the gentile, Cornelius. Through these encounters, the apostle learns that what he once thought to be God's intended order: namely, the separation of the clean from the unclean, the Jew from the gentile, is contrary to the divine order intended by God.[39] We see this, again, in the life of Jesus, as he regularly challenges the given societal and religious norms believed to align with God's holy order. Performing miracles on the Sabbath, touching the sick, speaking with a Samaritan woman, even healing a hemorrhaging woman who is rendered unclean by her constant bleeding: each of these an example of proper religious or social order that Jesus undermines with his actions.

In the last instance, we are told, in the book of Mark, that the woman had suffered constant bleeding for twelve years, a state that would have left her perpetually impure and, in turn, precluded her from full participation

38. One can apply the same logic to the Reconstruction and Jim Crow Era trope of the hypersexual Black man threatening the purity of the White, Christian woman. Once again, women's purity must be safeguarded from disorderly corruption by the Black man in order to maintain properly ordered (White) Christian society.

39. Acts 10:1–48.

within properly ordered society for more than a decade.[40] Given her marginal and contaminated status, it is noteworthy that Jesus is not upset by her proximity. He does not call for her removal from the gathered crowd, as would be correct according to the Levitical rules for the female discharge of blood.[41] He does not concern himself with the threat to individual purity or societal order that her bodily dysfunction poses. Instead, Jesus makes a point of stopping, in view of the entire crowd gathered around him, to inquire who has touched his cloak. In choosing to see and encounter the woman in this visible way, he publicly challenges the exclusionary practices rooted in what was thought to be proper, divinely ordained societal order.

Whether by associating with prostitutes or forgoing traditional washing rituals, Jesus regularly disregards the established purity practices of his day and, by doing so, undermines the system of order to which they belong. Throughout Scripture, God undermines our efforts to protect ourselves, to protect Christianity, and to protect the future of the kingdom through methods of exclusion and control predicated upon our own mistaken conception of proper order. Confronting our definition of right order, drawn from our reading of the Law, Jesus reveals and invites us into the truth of God's divine *oikonomia*. This holy economy into which Jesus calls us is not built upon stringent rules, rigid boundaries, exclusionary social practices, or feelings of fear and shame, but upon the divine relational economy of the triune God, who is always *with and for the other*.

Purity Through Participation

The economy of God is marked by the relational way of being *with and for the other*, because God, in and of Godself as immanent Trinity, is *with and for the other*.[42] As the second person of the Trinity, God, in Christ, takes on the fullness of our humanity, choosing to dwell among us and, thereby, bridging the ontological gulf between the infinite and the finite. By taking the materiality of our fleshly bodies, God reveals Godself to be *pro nobis*

40. Mark 5:24–36.

41. Haber, "Woman's Touch," 175–77. For a fascinating account of the development on *niddah* and the connection of menstruation with otherness in the Middle Ages, see Koren, "Menstruant as 'Other' in Medieval Judaism and Christianity."

42. For more on the social implications of the Trinity, see Wong, "Social Trinitarianism Through Iconic Participation."

(for us).[43] It is this very order, this way of being with and for the other, that Jesus manifests in his own life and that he teaches his followers. Moreover, it is this very order that marks the space of his body: "This is my body, broken for you."[44] In and through his body, Jesus offers to us the holy order of God, because Jesus *is* the holy order of God.

But this, of course, is not only who God is for us. As Dietrich Bonhoeffer notes, this way of being with and for the other, this way of ordering self in relation to the world, is the relational order to which we, too, are called.[45] This holy relationality that we are being asked to embody transgresses the limits that otherwise separate us from one another. For Christ, this looks like crossing ontological, religious, and societal boundaries to live out the divine relational economy. For humanity, this looks like transgressive participation in the divine economy, such that there is no longer a hierarchical division of male from female, Jew from gentile, slave from free. While particularity and diversity remain good aspects of our created state; the judgment, hostility, and fear that separate us according to sex, gender, sexuality, ethnicity, race, nationality, and socioeconomics are rendered moot within Christ—that is to say, within the righteous order of the kingdom.

Within the space of Christ's body, marked by this alternative relationality, purity is no longer to be understood as strict adherence to a set of ethical rules or the rigorous maintenance of exclusionary boundaries. No longer is righteousness before God determined by whether or not one follows specific purity laws. As the book of Hebrews tells us, with the sacrifice of Christ, the Law has come to be written upon our hearts and minds.[46] Rather than from strict adherence to certain rules and regulations, purity now stems from our ever-deepening transgressive participation in the divine economy that defines Christ's body, bringing our selves and our ways into accordance with the relational rhythms of God's holy order. Thus understood, our strivings after purity and proper order are shown to be small and petty in light of the sacred, relational logic of the divine.

The church has long concerned itself with the purity of women's bodies and bodily practices out of a praiseworthy desire to safeguard the Christian community from corruption. We have taught women that, in order to remain righteous and aligned with the ways of God, their bodies

43. Bonhoeffer, *Christ the Center*, 47–48.

44. 1 Cor 11:24 NIV.

45. Bonhoeffer, *Creation and Fall*, 58–60, 91–92.

46. Heb 10:14–16.

and embodiment must be strictly controlled, both through their own self-disciplinary postures and the disciplinary actions of others. And yet, to be a people ordered in accordance with God's will does not require the evaluative categorization, control, or exclusion of that which we have deemed disorderly or impure. It does not require constant policing of boundaries and bodies, whether our own or those of others.

The Spirit at Pentecost reveals to us that the kingdom is not realized through exclusionary methods intended to maintain a distinction between holy and unholy, pure and impure.[47] Instead of the careful policing of boundaries, the community of God is constituted through a Spirit-filled, open-handed transgression of the given limits of belonging that makes room for new encounters. It is through such unexpected and uncontrollable encounters that God creates something radically different and even more expansive than what has gone before. This is the order of God—this way of being with and for those who are different from us, with and for those we once thought outsiders, with and for those we once imagined to be impure. Our job is not to preserve and control, but to remain open as we are drawn further into the radically transgressive order of God and, through such participation, transformed accordingly. In such transformation, God reveals to us a more profound way of being, a more profound way of connecting, and a more profound way of embodying purity.

Bibliography

Albert the Great. *Questions Concerning Aristotle's* On Animals. Translated by Irven M. Resnick and Kenneth F. Kitchell Jr. Fathers of the Church, Mediaeval Continuation 9. Washington: Catholic University of America Press, 2008.

Aristotle. *Generation of Animals*. Translated by Arthur Leslie Peck. Loeb Classical Library. Cambridge: Harvard University Press, 1942.

———. *The Works of Aristotle*. Edited by William David Ross. Oxford: Clarendon, 1908–1931.

Aquinas. *The Summa Theologiae*. Translated by Fathers of the English Dominican Province. Rev. ed. 1920. New Advent, 2017. https://www.newadvent.org/summa/.

Augustine. *On the Trinity*. In vol. 3 of *The Nicene and Post-Nicene Fathers*, Series 1 (*NPNF*[1]). Edited by Philip Schaff. 1886-1889. Repr., Peabody, MA: Hendrickson, 1999.

Balmer, Randall. "The Religious Right and the Abortion Myth." *Politico*, May 10, 2022. https://www.politico.com/news/magazine/2022/05/10/abortion-history-right-white-evangelical-1970s-00031480.

Bonhoeffer, Dietrich. *Christ the Center*. San Francisco: HarperOne, 1978.

47. Acts 2:1–21.

———. *Creation and Fall: A Theological Exposition of Genesis 1–3*. Minneapolis: Fortress, 2004.

Coakley, John W. "The Powers of Holy Women." Chap. 1 in *Women, Men, and Spiritual Power: Female Saints and Their Male Collaborators*, 7–24. New York: Columbia University Press, 2006.

Gregory of Nyssa. *Ascetical Works*. Translated by Virginia Woods Callahan. Washington, DC: The Catholic University of America Press, 1999.

Haber, Susan. "A Woman's Touch: Feminist Encounters with the Hemorrhaging Woman in Mark 5.24–34." *Journal for the Study of the New Testament* 26 (2003) 171–92. https://doi.org/10.1177/0142064X0302600203.

Hauerwas, Stanley. "Abortion Theologically Understood (1991)." In *The Hauerwas Reader*, edited by John Berkman and Michael G. Cartwright, 603–22. Durham: Duke University Press, 2001.

Horowitz, Maryanne Cline. "Aristotle and Woman." *Journal of the History of Biology* 9 (1976) 183–213.

Howard, Katherine. "Female Saints and the Performance of Virginity in the Medieval Period." *Seattle University Undergraduate Research Journal* 6 (2022) 72–88. https://scholarworks.seattleu.edu/cgi/viewcontent.cgi?article=1259&context=suurj.

Johnson, Willis. "The Myth of Jewish Male Menses." *Journal of Medieval History* 24 (1998) 273–95.

Karras, Ruth Mazo. *Sexuality in Medieval Europe: Doing Unto Others*. 2nd ed. London: Routledge, 2012.

Koren, Sharon Faye. "The Menstruant as 'Other' in Medieval Judaism and Christianity." *Nashim: A Journal of Jewish Women's Studies and Gender Issues* 17 (2009) 33–59.

Lloyd, Genevieve. "The Man of Reason." *Metaphilosophy* 10 (1979) 18–37.

Lohr, Charles H. *St. Thomas Aquinas,* Scriptum Super Sententiis*: An Index of Authorities Cited*. Amersham, England: Avebury, 1980.

Merback, Mitchell, ed. *Beyond the Yellow Badge: Anti-Judaism and Antisemitism in Medieval and Early Modern Visual Culture*. Leiden: Brill, 2008.

Mondzain, Marie-Jose. *Image, Icon, Economy: The Byzantine Origins of the Contemporary Imaginary*. Stanford: Stanford University Press, 2004.

Mosedale, Susan Sleeth. "Science Corrupted: Victorian Biologists Consider 'The Woman Question.'" *Journal of the History of Biology* 11 (1978) 1–55.

Nolan, Michael. "The Aristotelian Background to Aquinas's Denial That 'Woman Is a Defective Male.'" *The Thomist: A Speculative Quarterly Review* 64 (2020) 21–69.

Resnick, Irven M. *Marks of Distinction: Christian Perceptions of Jews in the High Middle Ages*. Washington, DC: The Catholic University of America Press, 2012.

Shellnutt, Kate. "White Evangelicals Twice as Likely to Want to Ban Abortion." *Christianity Today*, May 6, 2022. https://www.christianitytoday.com/news/2022/may/abortion-legal-evangelicals-supreme-court-pew-research.html.

Soerens, Matthew. "This Love of Guns: It's Way Beyond Our Understanding." *The Better Samaritan with Kent Annan and Jamie Aten*. Podcast. *Christianity Today*. June 8, 2022.

Tasca, Cecilia, et al. "Women and Hysteria in the History of Mental Health." *Clinical Practice and Epidemiology in Mental Health* 8 (2012) 110–19.

Villarreal, Silvia, et al. *Gun Violence in the United States 2022: Examining the Burden Among Children and Teens*. Johns Hopkins Center for Gun Violence Solutions. Johns

Hopkins Bloomberg School of Public Health, 2024. https://publichealth.jhu.edu/sites/default/files/2024-09/2022-cgvs-gun-violence-in-the-united-states.pdf.

Wong, Jessica Wai-Fong. *Disordered: The Holy Icon and Racial Myths.* Waco, TX: Baylor University Press, 2021.

———. "Social Trinitarianism Through Iconic Participation." In *T&T Clark Handbook of Political Theology*, edited by Rubén Rosario Rodriguez, 900–902. London: T&T Clark, 2019.

Part II

Re-Constructing Evangelism

Chapter 6

Mission as Transformation

Al Tizon and Ruth Padilla DeBorst

The International Fellowship for Mission as Transformation, or INFEMIT, represents most directly a movement within the global Evangelical community that has championed the centrality of peace and justice on the missionary agenda, but with no intention whatsoever to decenter evangelism. That said, contrary to a reductionist definition of evangelism as the verbal communication of the gospel for the purpose of conversion, evangelism can be defined as embodied invitation to confess Jesus as Savior and Lord and to join the new community. It is bearing witness to the good news of the kingdom of God in word, deed, and life. Personal and social transformation, soul and society, evangelism and social engagement: the reintegration of these dimensions of the gospel defines holistic or integral mission. INFEMIT has been on the forefront of this movement, which has assumed the name, Mission as Transformation (MT). This chapter briefly reviews INFEMIT's history and commitments, and in so doing assesses the relevance of the Transformational movement for today.

History and Formation

The roots of INFEMIT can be traced to the response of a group of Evangelicals from around the globe, primarily from the non-Western world, who were at once jubilant about how social concern was affirmed at Lausanne 1 in 1974 but confused about how it continued to maintain secondary status on the Evangelical mission agenda in subsequent years. Their fears that the sociopolitical dimension of the gospel would be relegated perpetually to the margins were confirmed at a Lausanne follow-up consultation that convened in Pattaya, Thailand, in 1980. As its organizers pushed the agenda of unreached people groups, sociopolitical concern was not only regarded as secondary; some even called it a distraction to the real work of the gospel.

In their disappointment for the way the Thailand consultation went, a group of radical Evangelicals "resolved to meet . . . as a Two Thirds World consultation." Making good on their promise, the first of many gatherings convened in Bangkok in 1982. Framed and organized for the first time by theologians of Evangelical conviction from the majority world, they reflected together on the theme, "Sharing Jesus in the Two-Thirds World." This gathering led to the formation of a loose global network called the International Fellowship of Evangelical Mission Theologians, or INFEMIT.

Although 1987 marks the year when INFEMIT officially formed, 1980 claims its true beginnings when this group of radical Evangelicals at Pattaya in 1980 reacted strongly against what they considered a regrettable return to pre-Lausanne mission thinking. They began to come to terms with the fact that the brand of holistic mission theology they espoused will probably never flow into the mainstream of Evangelical missionary consciousness as long as "managerial missiology," as Samuel Escobar described it, dictated the current.

Names and institutions associated with this network early on would include Vinay Samuel and Chris Sugden at the Oxford Centre for Mission Studies in the United Kingdom; René Padilla, Samuel Escobar, and Orlando Costas of the Latin American Theological Fraternity; Melba Maggay of the Institute for Studies in Asian Church and Culture in the Philippines and David Lim of China Ministries International and Centre for Community Transformation, also in the Philippines; David Gitari and Kwame Bediako of the African Theological Fraternity based in both Kenya and Ghana; Peter Kuzmič of the Evangelical Theological Seminary in Osijek, Croatia; Ronald J. Sider of Evangelicals for Social Action; and many others.

Through many gatherings, publications, and collaborative actions, INFEMIT made a significant impact on maturing a Transformational vision for Evangelicals. Despite starts and stops, its work continues in and through the next generation of Evangelical theologian-practitioners. Now called the International Fellowship for Mission as Transformation, INFEMIT articulates its mission in the following way: "Called and equipped by the Father, Son and Holy Spirit, we are a gospel-centered fellowship of mission theologian-practitioners that serves local churches and other Christian communities so we together embody the kingdom of God through transformational engagement, both locally and globally."

If MT was born with the formation of INFEMIT in 1980, then its name formed at the Wheaton Consultation in 1983. Compared to Lausanne '74, the Wheaton '83 Consultation could not boast of huge numbers of participants nor of monumental worldwide notoriety. But in terms of the Evangelical journey toward holistic mission, Wheaton '83 looms large. Organized into three tracks, Track II of Wheaton '83, with the sub-theme "The Church in Response to Human Need," took significant strides toward holistic mission by developing a biblical, theological, and practical understanding of the term "transformation." According to the Wheaton '83 Statement, the official document resulting from Track II, "Transformation is the change from a condition of human existence contrary to God's purposes to one in which people are able to enjoy fullness of life in harmony with God."[1]

This particular understanding of transformation has undergone its own transformations since its inception. It emerged through reflections on social ethics but later expanded into reflections on a holistic missiology; thus, the name expansion to Mission as Transformation. This broadening, however, did not reduce the importance of social concern; on the contrary, it made social concern part and parcel of the gospel and therefore part and parcel of the church's mission. Proponents of MT refuse to understand evangelization without liberation, a change of heart without a change of structures, vertical reconciliation (between God and people) without horizontal reconciliation (between people and people), and church planting without community building. They point to the biblical paradigm of the reign or kingdom of God as the source and driver for this holistic understanding of mission. Vinay Samuel's 1999 articulation of the term sums it up well; he wrote, "Transformation is to enable God's vision of society to be actualized in all relationships—social, economic and spiritual—so that God's will may be reflected in human society and his love be experienced by all communities, especially the poor."[2]

1. Samuel and Sugden, "Transformation," 257.

2. Samuel, "Mission as Transformation," 225.

A Contextual Movement

Core to MT has been its commitment to doing theology contextually, that is, theologizing that is shaped by the local contexts in which the gospel is being worked out. This was and is in contrast to simply assuming the rightness of versions of the gospel imported by dominant cultures through the missionary enterprise. All theology is contextual theology, which can be defined as the articulations, perspectives and lived experience related to God and God's purposes born out of particular contexts. As such, how can any theology not be contextual theology?

Contextualization then describes the intercultural process by which the Christian message takes shape within a given context, giving way to fresh, local, relevant articulations of the Christian message. In short, contextualization generates contextual theologies. Rather than defining contextualization as a one-way process of the missionary learning the ways of another culture in order to communicate the gospel more effectively, it is a reciprocal process wherein people of two or more cultures learn together how best to express the transcultural faith in radically local ways by committing to full engagement with one another. For INFEMIT, such a process has required a commitment to certain practices.

First, it has required deep listening to and engaging with voices from the majority world. The original INFEMIT leaders in fact regarded Western European and North American counterparts as "friends" rather than "members" of the fellowship in order to give primary place to voices historically muted by Western missionary conventions. This posture reflected the courage of INFEMIT's architects since it went against the grain of Evangelical mission practice, thus advancing the conversation regarding power dynamics across cultures. They maintained this posture toward their mission friends from the West until 2010 as "INFEMIT 2.0" was being forged by the second generation of leaders.

These leaders believed that the deep listening and engagement required for genuine contextualization to occur begins with them. These leaders, who call themselves the Networking Team, hail from many parts of the world, and they have been meeting by Zoom monthly and in-person annually for the last seventeen years and counting. Every meeting has begun with personal check-ins, living into the meaning of "fellowship," as well as nurturing a culture conducive for mutual transformation and gospel partnership across the miles. Though the Networking Team has a coordinator and the board has a chairperson, INFEMIT has shied away from appointing an executive director or creating the position of president in favor of contextual mutuality. Time will tell if the organization can be sustained by this intentionally loose structure.

A second practice in genuine contextualization has been allowing the issues of particular contexts to define the mission. Rather than taking at face value theologies worked out by churches and seminaries from dominant cultures, Transformationists ask, "What are the issues in the local context that the local church needs to address?" This question has occupied the INFEMIT constituency since the beginning. And the answers, alongside wrestling with the Scriptures, are what give shape to the theology and mission for that context. Such an approach often requires deviating from what is considered universal for the church, being willing to brave the backlash from those who have assumed that their theology of mission was the theology of mission, and getting involved in sociopolitical issues that impact the masses.

Examples of INFEMIT's efforts to address current realities in particular contexts include issuing the "Call to Biblical Faithfulness Amid the New Fascism" at the time of the first inauguration of Donald J. Trump as the president of the United States. INFEMIT has also been active in speaking out against the atrocities being played out among the Palestinians for the last two years at the time of this writing. It has also been proactive in establishing theological educational centers that are designed by, for, and among a particular people. Comunidad de Estudios Teologicos Interdisciplinarios (CETI) equips Christian leaders in Latin America to engage the faith in the context of Latin American realities. In Romania, a graduate program in theology was incorporated into the educational programs of Aurel Vlaicu University in Arad. Under the supervision of INFEMIT leaders in Romania, the program was and is a direct result of INFEMIT's philosophy of contextual theological education.

Indeed, Mission as Transformation was and continues to be a movement of contextualization, as it imitates "the missionary approach" of God who sent the Son to dwell among us.

Core Values

INFEMIT has recently identified eight features of MT that make up the core values of the movement. These features are at once descriptive and aspirational, that is, they describe Transformationists at their best, which in the real world is not always the case! With that caveat . . .

Relational

The first feature is the commitment to relationships. Mission as Transformation is relational. That is, it is built on the conviction that relationships or friendships are at the core of the gospel and therefore the core of the mission of the gospel. If whatever we would deem an accomplishment in mission leaves a trail of broken relationships within organizations and/or with host cultures, then something went wrong. We would have missed the mark of true Christ-centered mission. This commitment to relationships emphasizes people over task and friendship over professionalism.

Spiritual

Another feature is the movement's Spiritual grounding. I capitalize "Spiritual" because I refer to the person of the Holy Spirit and not to a generic notion of what it means to be spiritual. MT seeks to be Spirit-led, and it does this in at least two ways. Firstly, worship and mission are regarded as two sides of the same coin; they are as inseparable as the two loves of the Great Commandment. As worship expresses our love commitment to God, mission expresses our love for our neighbors, near and far. Secondly, the arts play a crucial role in MT. Doing mission requires dependence on the creative, beautiful, transforming power of the Holy Spirit. Through song, dance, visual arts, creative liturgies, and many other artistic expressions, MT affirms whole-being engagement—head, heart, and hands, in contradistinction to the over-intellectualization of theology. What role does *poiesis* play in mission? How does taking seriously the affective and intuitive sides of our beings impact the theology and practice of mission? Transformationists ask such questions in their quest to bear witness to the creative, transforming work of the Holy Spirit in the world.

Integral

To be integral is a third feature, which can be regarded as the founding core value of MT. To be integral is to strive in the Spirit to be faithful to the full implications of the gospel. It challenges the propensity of the church to emphasize one dimension of the gospel at the expense of another. Though there have been important convergences over the last sixty years, enough that the evangelism versus social concern debate could be considered done, the consequences of the infamous fundamentalist-modernist split within North American Protestantism linger. Many churches and mission agencies continue to struggle with maintaining a holistic or integral mission in their theology and practice. It is against the backdrop of this ongoing challenge that INFEMIT and other transformational agencies continue to promote and live out an integral mission.

Contextual

To be contextual is another founding feature of MT. It takes with utmost seriousness the cultural and social context of a given location for the proper doing of theology in that location. Fortunately, the idea that all theology is contextual theology is now widely accepted, at least on the theoretical level. Much has still to be advanced in terms of the church's missionary practice in this area. One of the strongest missional calls of contextual theology today is for the global church to interrogate and repudiate paternalism, ethnocentrism, racism, and all other isms of colonial-style mission.

Preferential Option for the Poor

Its adherence to the idea of God's preferential option for the poor constitutes another core value. The poor, broadly defined as including all who suffer levels of deprivation physically, personally, sociopolitically, economically, psycho-emotionally, morally, spiritually, and any combination thereof, are often who are overlooked in conventional theological discourse. In contrast, they are at the center of MT, as Transformationists locate the ministry of Jesus deeply among the poor, oppressed, marginalized, and traumatized of his day. Jesus himself said that he came to preach the gospel to the poor (Luke 4:18). Matthew 9:35–39 aptly describes Christ's ministry, going about, "all the cities and villages, teaching in their synagogues, and proclaiming the good news of the kingdom, and curing every disease and every sickness" (NRSVue). Along with the liberationists, Transformationists have been radically touched by God's heart for the poor to which the ministry of Jesus testifies, and they seek to do what Jesus did in the power of the Spirit.

Ecclesial

Another feature is the commitment to the church, both universally, affirming the unity of the worldwide communion, and locally, affirming the practical, manifold ways in which local congregations engage in mission. Universally speaking, the church is one in all its diverse glory, and by its unity bears witness to the power of the gospel. In that light, working toward unity across genders, races, ethnicities, cultures, generations, traditions, and theological distinctions is missional, and it is worth striving for in the Spirit. MT has always been committed to the mission of unity, as it has cooperated with groups ranging from the Lausanne Movement to the World Council of Churches.

Locally, MT believes that the visible, local community of Christ constitutes the basic missional unit of transformation. The local congregation is God's foundational change agent. Mission agencies, humanitarian, activist and nonprofit organizations, and denominations should emerge from local churches and exist to serve local churches in mission. Transformationists affirm the central role that the local church plays in God's mission.

Ecumenical

Related to being ecclesial, MT is also ecumenical; that is, it affirms the bigness of God's church and is willing to partner with all who are doing God's work in the world. This goes beyond merely being interdenominational to being inter-traditional, going beyond beyond the Evangelical tradition and working with Roman Catholics, Orthodox, and non-Evangelical Protestants. It also means an openness to interfaith dialogue and seeks peace across religions in a world where religious wars are on the rise.

Praxiological

Lastly, it is praxiological; that is, it is committed to the dynamic cycle of action and reflection, pastoral and missional practice, and theological reflection working together for the transformation of the world. The church is once again indebted to Liberationists who introduced the praxis model of doing theology. To be praxiological means to take seriously the two mutually benefiting sides of action and reflection. A conventional educational approach would be illustrated by a straight line, where students learn theories and principles, graduate, and then spend the rest of their lives applying what they learned, at best, with annual ongoing educational requirements. The praxis model brings the two ends of the line together and forms a circle, so instead of theory simply impacting practice, the cyclical nature of education has practice also impacting theory. Paulo Freire's definition of praxis aptly sums it up for theology and mission. He defines praxis as "action and reflection" upon the world "in order to transform it."[3]

These eight features of Mission as Transformation—1) integral; 2) contextual; 3) relational; 4) Spiritual; 5) preferential option for the poor; 6) ecclesial; 7) ecumenical; and 8) praxiological—make up the movement's core values. Is a movement that holds these core values to the theology and practice of mission still needed, or has it run its course? Was Mission as Transformation "a period piece," an exotic paradigm of mission forged by a handful of Evangelical mavericks from yesteryear that can now be shelved?

At the time of this writing, the fourth Lausanne Congress had just recently convened in Seoul, South Korea. INFEMIT leader Ruth Padilla DeBorst was invited by Lausanne to speak on the theme of justice and was given fifteen minutes to do so. Lausanne's desire to cover a wide range of mission-related issues prevented the organizers from committing any more time than that. Though INFEMIT found it problematic that justice was just another issue among many, Padilla DeBorst accepted the invitation.

Even in those brief fifteen minutes, her words managed to stir controversy among the delegates, enough that an official apology was issued, leaving many within the transformational community baffled, confused, and even shocked. Padilla DeBorst's controversial words had to do with the situation in Palestine as an example of an injustice occurring in the world today. And the sparks flew! The unfolding of this incident has been reported by several media outlets, including *Sojourners*, *Christian Post*, and others. INFEMIT's concern was not limited to giving the theme of justice just fifteen minutes at the largest ever Evangelical missionary gathering; its concern also included the fact that calling the genocide occurring in Palestine as an injustice was controversial!

3. Freire, *Pedagogy of the Oppressed*, 66.

I bring up what happened at Lausanne to emphasize the absolute need for voices like INFEMIT's to continue to speak and speak loudly. The gospel has something vital to say about human suffering due to sociopolitical injustice, and when we engage in alleviating the suffering, we bear witness to the gospel. Justice is central to the church's witness to the good news of Jesus Christ in the world; it is part and parcel of our evangelistic efforts. Wherever wars rage; wherever people fall victim to sexism, racism, classism, and all other -isms; wherever bully dictators abuse their power and crush the vulnerable; and wherever life and the dignity of life are threatened, the church of Jesus Christ needs to be there as bearers of the gospel, embodying the justice, peace, righteousness, and love of God.

Bibliography

Freire, Paulo. *Pedagogy of the Oppressed.* Translated by Myra Bergman Ramos. New York: Herder and Herder, 1972.

Samuel, Vinay, and Christopher Sugden, eds. *The Church in Response to Human Need: Papers from the Consultation on the Church in Response to Human Need, Held in Wheaton, Ill., in June 1983 and Sponsored by the World Evangelical Fellowship.* Grand Rapids: Eerdmans 1987.

Samuel, Vinay and Chris Sugden, eds. *Mission as Transformation: A Theology of the Whole Gospel.* Oxford: Regnum Books International, 1999.

Chapter 7

Evangelism Among People of Other Faiths

Jose Abraham, Darren Duerksen, and Vinod John

Evangelism is a term fraught with controversy in postcolonial and post-Christian societies like ours, burdened by its historical association with colonialism. Historically, European missionaries utilized evangelism as a tool to denigrate local cultures and traditions, aligning their efforts with the broader colonial agenda of civilizing missions. As contemporary societies work towards decolonizing perspectives, there's a growing need to reassess the implications of evangelism and shed its colonial legacy. Our panel aims to explore and redefine evangelism in a way that is sensitive to our modern context. We seek to address how we can effectively share the good news of Jesus Christ while honoring and respecting the diverse cultural and religious sensibilities present in today's world. Evangelism should celebrate, rather than undermine, the rich cultural traditions that are a divine gift. Sharing the good news of Jesus Christ in multicultural, post-colonial societies demands the contextualization of the gospel in the language and idioms of the people, engaging with them on issues of common good and justice, relating at an affective level, and serving others on their terms for mutual enrichment. Consequently, evangelism in a culturally and religiously pluralistic world should embrace a wide range of practices, including friendship, witnessing, hospitality, interfaith dialogue, and social activism. Within this broader conversation, Vinod John will discuss evangelism among "caste Hindus" in North India, while Darren Duerksen will address challenges faced in outreach to Sikhs. Although our focus is not on other non-Christian communities, the insights from these discussions are intended to have broad applicability and relevance.

India, with a population surpassing 1.3 billion, stands as the most populous country in the world. It is a cradle for major religious traditions including Hinduism, Buddhism, Sikhism, and Jainism, and has also been a fertile ground for Islam, Christianity, and Judaism since their inception. Beyond its multireligious landscape, India is a mosaic of multiculturalism, hosting hundreds of distinct cultures and thousands of unique communities, each with its own culinary traditions, costumes, and languages. Indeed, India's diversity extends to its linguistic profile, boasting over twenty-five official languages, making it much more than a country in the European sense—it is a subcontinent rich in traditions and customs. This cultural and linguistic diversity positions India as a unique entity on the global stage, currently ranked as the fifth largest economy in the world. Despite its economic stature, India grapples with significant challenges, including widespread poverty and a complex caste system that includes numerous castes and sub-castes. This diversity and complexity render evangelism a particularly challenging task within the nation. In such a diverse setting, a single interpretation of the gospel cannot universally resonate as good news for every community. Therefore, the gospel needs to be interpreted and presented in various ways to align with the distinct sensibilities of different communities. This approach is essential for evangelism to be meaningful and effective in India's multifaceted social and cultural landscape.

Christianity in India boasts a rich history that spans nearly 2000 years, tracing back to the first century CE when it is believed that the Apostle Thomas brought the Christian faith to the southwest province of Kerala. For many centuries, the Christian community in Kerala remained small and relatively contained until significant changes occurred with the arrival of European traders and missionaries. The landmark arrival of Vasco da Gama in 1498 marked the introduction of Roman Catholic Christianity to India. The Portuguese actively sought to convert local populations, sometimes using coercive methods that intertwined religious conversion with the broader goals of economic and territorial control. The conquest-driven violent Christianity of the Portuguese clashed with existing Christians in India. The landscape of Indian Christianity underwent another major transformation in the nineteenth century with the arrival of British missionaries, who introduced Protestant Christianity. These missionaries primarily focused their efforts on the Dalit community, who were particularly receptive to the gospel. This receptivity can be attributed to the social and spiritual upliftment that Christianity promised, contrasting sharply with the rigid caste hierarchical structures they traditionally faced. The Christian message of equality and brotherhood held particular appeal to the Dalits, offering a promise of spiritual liberation and social upliftment. Protestant missions were instrumental in establishing schools, hospitals, and social service institutions, which played a crucial role in community development and were attractive to those who were socially and economically disadvantaged. The impact of these missionary activities was profound, leading to significant conversions among the Dalit communities. Today, the legacy of these missions is evident, as Dalit Christians represent a substantial proportion of the Christian population in India. However, the colonial legacy of Christianity resulted in the perception that Christianity is a tradition advanced through conquest, and gains through illicit means.

Religious and caste identities are deeply ingrained in Indian society, with every individual typically associated with a specific caste. This caste identity is not easily altered and remains a significant factor in social stratification. Caste mobility, although possible under certain conditions, is limited, and the complete abolition of caste seems unattainable. The resilience of the caste system is often reinforced by Hindu religious myths, which legitimize and perpetuate the hierarchy. For Dalits, who are situated at the lowest echelon of the social hierarchy, caste identity imposes severe limitations and perpetuates discrimination. Historically, remaining within the Hindu fold meant that Dalits had little opportunity to challenge or escape this discrimination. As a result, many Dalits turned to Christianity, driven by the efforts of Christian missionaries who offered an alternative to the oppressive caste system. Conversion was seen as a path to liberation from caste-imposed identities and inequalities. However, even though converting to Christianity provided some relief, it did not entirely free Dalits from discrimination. Within the broader hierarchical social order of India, converted Dalits often continue to face marginalization, albeit in different forms. Due to the significant social implications of changing one's religious and thus caste identity, religious conversion is viewed with suspicion and often contested in India. This suspicion is linked to broader concerns about identity change, which is a contentious issue in the context of conversion and evangelism. The potential for religious conversion to disrupt traditional caste configurations makes it a focal point of social tension. In this complex interplay of religion and social structure, religious conversion is not merely a personal spiritual decision but a profound shift in social identity that can have wide-reaching implications.

In India, religious conversion transcends mere spiritual transformation and is deeply entwined with political and social dynamics. Several Indian states have enacted anti-conversion laws aimed primarily at curbing conversions from Hinduism to Christianity or Islam. These laws require converts to report to the police if they are converting. These laws are indicative of the sensitive nature of religious identity in India, where conversion is often perceived as a threat to the societal order and cultural continuity. Consequently, both individuals who facilitate conversions and those who convert face penalties under these laws, highlighting the contentious nature of religious freedom in the country. This legal and social framework is set against a backdrop of rising Hindutva politics, which champions Hindu supremacy and sees conversions to other faiths as diluting the Hindu character of the nation. In this environment, religious persecution has become increasingly common, further complicating the practice of evangelism. A significant challenge for missionaries and religious reformers, therefore, is how to approach the issue of evangelism without coercing people to change their religious identity—a change that carries heavy social and legal implications. The question then arises: Can conversion be conceptualized merely as a change of heart that does not necessitate a disruption of one's social identity? This perspective would be particularly crucial for caste Hindus, for whom conversion can imply not just a religious shift but also a potential estrangement from their social roots. In his presentation, Vinod John explores this nuanced issue, proposing that evangelism can be conducted in a manner that respects individual choice and cultural heritage, thus redefining conversion as an internal spiritual journey rather than a complete transformation of social identity. This approach seeks to mitigate the tensions associated with conversion, offering a path forward that aligns spiritual enrichment with cultural integrity.

Given the intricate sociopolitical and caste dynamics in India, evangelism extends far beyond the traditional realms of preaching and teaching the gospel of Jesus Christ. Darren Duerksen has emphasized the importance of engaging in both orthopraxy (right action) and orthopathy (right feeling) when interacting with people of other faiths. In a society marked by significant economic disparities, the role of social work and activism becomes crucial. As Christians, there is a compelling need to collaborate with people from different religious backgrounds and those working in non-profit organizations to address issues of common good and justice. Such collaborations can help build trust among communities that might otherwise view Christianity with suspicion, seeing it as a foreign or colonial imposition rather than a genuinely local and integrated faith. This mistrust has historical roots, as the association of Christian missionaries with British colonialism has led to a lasting skepticism towards Christians and their evangelistic efforts in India. Despite the substantial contributions of Christians to educational and health services in the country, overcoming the stigma of colonial association remains a significant challenge. Working alongside others not only helps in addressing critical social issues but also paves the way for a more inclusive understanding of Christianity. By demonstrating a commitment to the welfare of all community members, irrespective of their religious affiliations, Christians in India can foster a more nuanced appreciation of their faith as a relevant and integral part of Indian society, rather than an external or alien influence. This approach to evangelism, rooted in practical love and service, offers a promising path forward in bridging divides and building lasting relationships across diverse communities.

Case Study 1: Redeeming Intercultural Evangelism Among Hindus Today

The commencement of Jesus Christ's ministry was marked by the proclamation of the good news of the kingdom of God, accompanied by an exhortation for individuals to repent and undergo a transformation of heart (Mark 1:14–15; Matt 4:17), a process commonly referred to as conversion. However, the concept of conversion to Christianity, encompassing baptism and the subsequent sociocultural displacement of converts in certain regions, has long been a subject of contention particularly for caste Hindus.

The Hindu caste system has historically perpetuated the marginalization of outcastes or untouchables, now self-identifying as Dalits, relegating them to the lowest stratum of society with no prospects for upward social mobility. Consequently, when presented with the gospel, Dalits eagerly embraced the potential for socioeconomic and religious amelioration offered by conversion to Christianity. They willingly chose to depart from their oppressive social existence. In numerous instances, Dalits actively sought out Christian communities or mission compounds in pursuit of social equality and dignity. Indeed, Dalits had nothing to lose except their oppressive shackles and long-standing subjugation, as Lancy Lobo aptly stated, "The untouchables were in search of equality and betterment of their status by escaping from the tyranny, rigidity, exploitation, and oppression they suffered."[1]

Conversely, the situation differed significantly for educated caste Hindus, who enjoyed privileged positions and numerous societal benefits. For this group, accepting the gospel and converting implied relinquishing their elevated status within the community to join Christian congregations predominantly composed of so-called "impure" mass converts from outcastes and indigenous tribes. Consequently, caste Hindus have maintained a persistent aversion to conversion to Christianity.

This dichotomy prompted me to investigate the underlying reasons for caste Hindus' resistance to evangelism and the Christian call for conversion, leading to ethnographic research conducted in Varanasi, North India. The evangelistic approach of E. Stanley Jones, a prominent twentieth-century American Methodist missionary in India who felt particularly called to evangelize educated caste Hindus, had influenced my research to go in this direction. My ethnographic study involved interviews with over 250 caste Hindus who profess faith in Jesus Christ as their Lord while maintaining their Hindu identity. These firsthand interactions, coupled with my personal experience, suggest that intercultural evangelism among caste Hindus necessitates a differentiated approach compared to other people groups in India. This distinction is warranted by the historical and sociocultural realities of the Indian subcontinent.

The Historical Setting

The late nineteenth and early twentieth centuries witnessed a significant period of Western imperialistic expansion, concurrent with an intensification of evangelistic efforts by foreign missionary societies in India. This convergence led to a conflation of evangelism with Western imperialism. As one historian has observed, despite the British government's "official policy of religious neutrality, . . . Christian missions appeared to be an arm of the British Raj."[2] This perception was viewed negatively by a growing

1. Lobo, "Visions and Illusions of Dalit Converts."

2. Quotation commonly cited in discussions of Christian missions and British rule in India; original author and publication information are unknown.

cohort of nationalistic Indians, resulting in a widespread association of colonialism with missionary activities among the general populace.

While British evangelism encompassed diverse ideological streams, there existed a broad consensus in both British imperialist and missionary policies towards India. Missionaries were expected to acknowledge the authority of the Raj and refrain from political engagement. In practice, for Indians, conversion entailed not only an inner spiritual transformation but also an overt declaration of allegiance to Christ and church membership. Baptism became the primary metric for evaluating the efficacy of evangelization, often overshadowing other efforts aimed at internal transformation. This evangelistic fervor occurred against the backdrop of political upheaval in early twentieth century, characterized by growing native demands for British withdrawal from India. European missionaries, for the most part, remained disengaged from the hopes and aspirations of the indigenous population, distancing themselves from public discourse. Consequently, Hindu communities often viewed converts as denationalized and unpatriotic, despite the active engagement of several prominent converts in the independence movement.

The mass-movements among Dalits and indigenous peoples. Despite concerted efforts, missionaries struggled to make significant inroads among educated caste Hindus, leading to a strategic shift in focus towards Dalits and indigenous peoples. This missionary reorientation precipitated a "mass movement" towards churches, driven by a complex interplay of socioeconomic and religiopolitical factors. The en masse conversions of Dalits, along with some Hindus, generated tensions within the broader Hindu community, as these were perceived as a form of communal aggression and a threat to Hindu religious identity. The ritual of baptism particularly came to symbolize a rupture with one's cultural past and assimilation into European cultural norms, burdening nascent Indian churches with a complex historical and missiological legacy.

The mass conversion phenomenon sparked a revulsion among caste-Hindus for the church's evangelism and conversion of outcastes. Leaders of the Indian nationalist movement, most notably Mahatma Gandhi, openly criticized mass conversions, accusing missionaries of exploiting the plight of the untouchables. Gandhi's opposition to conversion was rooted in the Hindu philosophical tenet of equality of religions and the belief that all religions were equal. However, it is noteworthy that Gandhi's primary objection was to proselytism—the changing of religious affiliations without concomitant spiritual transformation. He stated that India did not need conversion from one faith to another.[3] Most caste Hindus, today, subscribe to the view that all religions are equally valid and can be accommodated within their pantheon of beliefs. However, they object to conversion from Hinduism to Christianity, which is still perceived as a foreign (Western) religion and a threat to their social, religious, and cultural identity. Hindus perceive conversion as a superficial change in external affiliation motivated by ulterior considerations rather than a genuine spiritual transformation.

In this context, Jones developed a nuanced approach to evangelizing Hindus in India considering the complex socioreligious and political realities of his mission. Unlike many of his contemporaries, Jones recognized that Christianity in India was often associated with Western imperialism and the religious hegemony of the British Raj. He believed that the objective of Christian mission should not be to impose Western cultural norms and ecclesial structure on India, but rather to introduce Christ to Indian culture and allow Christ to work out an organic transformation of India's spiritual and cultural heritage.

Jones understood that evangelism that disregarded the growing national consciousness of Indians would ultimately prove ineffective. Consequently, he advocated for "evangelism among the educated Indians,"[4] seeing them as a neglected demographic potentially receptive to the gospel if their national aspirations were respected. This approach was significantly influenced by Jones' encounter with Mahatma Gandhi, during which Gandhi emphasized the importance of Christians embodying the life and teachings of Jesus Christ, practicing their religion without dilution, emphasizing love, and approaching non-Christian religions with empathy and understanding.

The aversion to conversion among certain people groups should not be construed as grounds for abandoning evangelism entirely, as some Christians have done. The intrinsic nature of the gospel necessitates its dissemination as we respond to humanity's needs. Therefore, the following considerations may contribute to the redemption of intercultural evangelism today:

1. Our approach to evangelism must transcend the traditional Evangelical understanding that focuses solely on evangelism as saving souls. As Jones had advocated, the motive and ultimate objective of Christian

3. Gandhi, *In Search of the Supreme*, 10.

4. Jones, "Evangelism Among the Educated Indians."

evangelism should be the cultivation of "Christ-like character." Jones emphasized the development of this character among his converts, viewing Jesus as the paradigm for human character. This approach prioritized genuine spiritual transformation and character development through sincere discipleship, rather than numerical growth, as a metric of evangelistic success.

2. Evangelism should endeavor to address Hindus profound needs and provide solutions to social, cultural, or political concerns. The evangelistic approach should eschew any sense of superiority, instead, presenting Christ and embodying the message preached. The reciprocal nature of evangelism must be acknowledged, recognizing that the process of "evangelism evangelizes the evangelist" as well. Jones's mission exemplifies this approach. His method of evangelizing Hindus in India, influenced by his encounter with Mahatma Gandhi and his understanding of the gospel's nature, demonstrated humility and authenticity. Jones emphasized considering the socioreligious and political context of his audience, respecting their culture and sociopolitical aspirations, and cultivating Christ-like character among those responsive to the gospel.

3. In evangelizing Hindus, it is imperative to differentiate Jesus Christ from organized Christianity, presenting Christ as grounded in personal experience rather than the Christ enshrined in ecclesial dogmas. The spiritual experiences of gospel recipients should be heeded and examined, rather than focusing on theological differences. This should lead to interreligious dialogue that is centered on an open and amicable exchange of spiritual perspectives, aiming to foster mutual learning and enrichment of faith. This approach to evangelism as spiritual dialogue is rooted in the ancient Hindu practice of *shastrarth*, and is more contextually appropriate for the Indian milieu compared to methods such as "Gospel Crusades," "Power Evangelism," "Evangelism Campaign," or "Evangelism Explosion," which some Christians continue to employ insensitively in evangelizing Hindus and Muslims.

4. In intercultural evangelism, emphasis should be placed on spiritual experiences rather than doctrines. Both Hindu philosophy and Indian Christian theology accord high regard to *anubhava* (experience) as a primary source of revelation. Adopting *anubhava* as the driving force of dialogues, whether in personal or formal public settings, involves

encouraging participants to share their distinct experiences and perceptions of spirituality or belief, without abstractions of the reality, and how these guide their daily lives. This approach fosters humility and acknowledges that the goal is not to win religious debates or promote a spirit of conquest and faith superiority, but to create mutual understanding and appreciation of spiritual experiences. Trusting in the work of the Holy Spirit in such evangelism can lead to transformative impacts on participants.

5. The caste Hindu people group remains largely neglected in terms of focused ministry and engagement with their specific issues, such as objections to baptism and apprehension towards belonging to an organized church. Personal ethnographic research in Varanasi, India, revealed that numerous caste Hindus are receptive to Jesus Christ and his teachings, with some even professing belief that He is their Lord and Savior. However, many either delay or refrain from baptism and choose to remain outside the institutional church. This missiological issue and the challenges it poses for evangelizing caste Hindus have yet to be seriously addressed by the church.

Case Study 2: Is the Gospel Good News or Threatening News to Sikhs?

As we think about evangelism to Sikhs, I would like to briefly discuss two realities, some signs of hope, and conclude with areas for growth.

First, however, we can acknowledge that many Western Christians are unfamiliar with the Sikh community and religious tradition. One reason is that Sikhism itself is a relatively recent and small community in relation to other religious groups. Sikhism itself began to emerge in the sixteenth century in the modern-day Indian state of Punjab, which continues to be the home for most Sikhs. Of the estimated twenty-six million Sikhs worldwide, twenty-four million live in Punjab, and the remaining two million are located primarily in Canada, the United Kingdom, and the United States. Many of these live in and around major cities like Vancouver and London, though many have also moved to rural areas.

The religious beliefs and practices of Sikhism share some similarities to aspects of Hinduism and Islam. However, though most Sikhs would acknowledge some similarities, they would also claim that theirs is a very distinct religious tradition. This emphasis on distinctiveness has arguably increased over the last 150 years, and continues to do so today, as the Sikh community has sought to defend itself against various religious, colonial, social, and political pressures.

This leads to one of the first realities that I would like to note regarding the Christian evangelism of Sikhs. Historically, and now, Sikhs view Christian evangelism as a threat. There are, of course, various reasons for this, but a common factor regards the disparity (real or perceived) of power. That is, Christian communities in and from the West have exercised power over Sikhs and other minority or colonized communities in a variety of ways. Of course, this power has often stemmed from other aspects of identity, racial, socioeconomic, and national identity (such as White, Middle-Class, American/European, etc.), and has taken economic, social, and political forms. In their evangelism efforts it has been common for Western Christians to take advantage of and use forms of this power, whether in communication (funding evangelism material, conferences, etc.), mission presence (funding mission trips and personnel), and other ways.

Of course, these uses of power and resource in and of themselves do not always create a sense of deep threat. If a group is evangelized by another group, and both share similar levels of power and resource, the group being evangelized will not usually experience the other as threatening their existence. But when there is a disparity in power between the two groups, along with a history of the dominant group (or parts of it) using its power to in some ways harm the other group and its identity, the sense of threat can be strong. This was illustrated in June 2023 when a London Sikh community came to know about a planned consultation on Christian ministry to Sikhs. The consultation was to be held at a Baptist church in a borough of London, and was hosted by various groups, including two groups of the Lausanne Movement. The promotional flyer was, in many ways, quite moderate in its tone. It did not use Evangelical evangelism language that some communities find inflammatory, such as "targeting," "convert," "strategy," etc. The speakers were all well-known South Asian Christian leaders, and the listed topics were simply "new beginnings," "new challenges," and "new horizons." It did title the consultation "National Sikh Consultation: Calling Sikhs to Christ," which the organizers later realized was perhaps not a helpful choice. But, in short, the advertisement was quite non-threatening, at least in the estimation of the organizers.

Nonetheless, several days before the consultation, some in the Sikh community, including a local Sikh leader and borough councilor, began to protest the event and discuss it in social media. The leader wrote, "All individuals, regardless of their faith, should have the freedom to practice their religion without fear of coercion or undue influence from external sources."[5] The implied concern was that the conference would stoke Christian fears about Sikhs and promote strategies of coercion. In light of the Sikh's concerns, and the lack of time to address them, the consultation leaders decided to cancel the event.

In the following days many Sikhs and Sikh journalists responded to and reflected on the event. Most strongly reacted against the idea of evangelization between religious communities, claiming that Sikhism does not condone evangelism and conversion. But it is particularly instructive to note how some connected modern day Christian evangelism among Sikhs to the nineteenth and early twentieth century missionary work among poorer Sikh communities in the Punjab, India. One Sikh journalist wrote, "There is . . . a long history of Christian missionaries acting in a predatory fashion, targeting those perceived as vulnerable, promising them miracles and sometimes even money. In the UK, such Christian conversion events prey on insecurities minority communities like Sikhs can have, which can stem from being the 'other' whilst living in a Christian country."[6]

It is not my purpose to discuss the long and ongoing debate regarding if or how Christian missionaries in India coerced poor and low-caste Hindus and Sikhs with promises of money, health care, and education, and if this continues today. Rather, this example suggests, along with many others, that Sikhs experience and talk about Christian evangelism through what I will call the Sikh persecution narrative.

Much has been written on the importance of persecution and struggle for the formation of Sikh identity. And it is certainly the case that, from its early years, Sikh communities were threatened by various forces. This took concrete form in the seventeenth and eighteenth century battles against the Mughals, and in the nineteenth century against Afghan and British forces. Modern-day Sikh communities often recount the stories of struggle, battles, martyrdom, perseverance, and triumph from these times. The stories they recount, however, are not only those of past centuries, but also of recent years. They recount stories such as Operation Blue Star, the 1984 assault by

5. "Christian Conversion Event Cancelled."

6. "Christian Conversion Event Cancelled."

Indian government forces on the Harmandir Sahib, or Sikh golden temple; an attack that resulted in the death of Sikh separatists and extensive damage to one of the Sikh community's most revered locations. They tell stories regarding the farm acts of 2020, bills passed by the Indian parliament that negatively targeted, or at least deeply handicapped, the ability of Punjabi and Sikh farmers to make a living. They also tell stories that extend beyond the Punjab in India, such as the June 2023 shooting of Hardeep Singh Nijjar in the city of Surrey in British Columbia, Canada. Nijjar was an outspoken critic of the Indian government and an activist for the creation of a separate Sikh state. When he was shot Sikhs immediately began to suspect and accuse the Indian government of executing him.

Sikhs are aware not only of political threats, but also those from religious groups. Whether it was the Hindu, Muslim, or Christian missionaries that sought to convert Sikhs in the nineteenth and twentieth centuries, or modern-day Christian evangelism programs, Sikhs are mindful of initiatives that, in their minds, seek to replace or destroy their invaluable cultural and religious practices and identities. And this, as I discussed above, directly impacts the way Sikhs experience Christian evangelism. For many Sikhs such initiatives are just the latest of over a century's efforts by Christians to dominate and eliminate them. Through this lens, the gospel is seen not as good news, but as threatening news.

This relates to the second challenge: the Christian expectation or requirement that Sikhs give up their Sikh identity, or important aspects of their identity, in order to follow Christ. I have written elsewhere about the desire of some persons to follow Jesus while still relating to their Sikh community. Some of these have shared that, in their understanding, the origins of Sikhism under their first guru, Guru Nanak, actually allowed for a wider range of faith expression than modern-day Sikhism accepts. In their minds the relatively recent Sikh emphasis on strong, clear religious boundaries that would try to keep Sikhs from following and prioritizing Jesus and the Bible is not fully consistent with the original spirit and intent of Guru Nanak.

Religious studies scholars have indeed noted ways in which Guru Nanak was influenced by the less-rigid devotional Sant and Bhakti traditions that had long been influential in north India. These traditions provided certain frameworks for the early gurus that they partially adopted. For instance, often individual Sant poets or leaders would gain disciples and establish camps, or *deras*. In the Sikh communities these *deras* were what eventually became known as gurdwaras, or Sikh centers for worship. But even as the Sikh movement coalesced more and more into a distinct tradition with its own practices, beliefs, and identity, *dera* subgroups continued to proliferate both within and outside of this tradition. For example, while the gurdwara eventually became its own established institution, other *dera* communities often developed as alternatives to these. Often these other *deras* emerged as reactions to the Sikh communities and institutions, such as the *dera* communities created by and for various Dalit castes.

In short, Sikhism grew up in, and continues to exist in, the midst of a *dera* culture. Modern-day *deras* share some similar characteristics to early Sikhism, while also innovating in their own way. Normally *deras* have at their center a charismatic leader—a baba—who is known for dynamic messages, healing, and other miracles. These communities also often feature interactive singing and foster devotion to a deity or guru. In this way *deras* often parallel and interrelate with Sikh and Hindu traditions and communities while also operating in a liminal place outside of the normal religious structures. Some Christ-following gatherings are, in many ways, operating within this culture and seeking to be like *deras*—groups of Christ-followers that operate alongside Sikh gurdwaras, Hindu temples, and even mainline Christian churches, without fully identifying with any of these. Not unlike Nanak and many other religious pioneers of the region, they are influenced by these, but also seek to resist some of the socioreligious pressures to conform to existing religious boundaries.

This resistance can take various forms. For example, Christ-followers will prioritize Jesus as God and the Bible as Scripture but will also continue to wear a turban and *kara*, or steel bangle. These are, of course, important symbols in Sikhism, and they are also important symbols of community and identity. Some also prefer styles of worship that feel similar to a Sikh gurdwara or *dera*, sitting on the floor while singing along with or listening quietly to music and listening to a teacher share from the Bible while sitting on a platform. This is because for Sikhs, the worship style and set-up of many Christian churches, including many Indian churches, does not reflect the reverence and respect they would expect as appropriate for worshiping God. As a personal example, one time while attending an Evangelical-style church in California I welcomed a Sikh family into our Christmas church service. I sat next to them and, as I viewed the service through their eyes, I became aware of the ways in which it must have appeared quite strange and unspiritual in comparison to a Sikh gurdwara. It is quite probable that, in their eyes, our service resembled an interactive concert and theater show, not a place where God was revered and worshiped. In light of this I was disappointed, but not completely surprised when they got up and left halfway through the service.

My point here is that in our evangelism, it is important to remember the importance of Sikh identity and spirituality and to be open to how Christ followers in and from Sikh communities may want to integrate their faith in Christ with their Sikh tradition and practices. In many ways, this impulse seeks to counter the narrative, prominent in India and many other contexts, that following Christ destroys one's identity, tradition, and community. It also, in many ways, de-constructs and then re-constructs parts of the modern framework of comparative religions where evangelism can quickly become a forum for competition between religions.

How can Christians maintain an evangelism that resists the narrative and pressure of competition and is attentive to the threats other religionists feel? I think there are signs of hope and possibility. One is the attraction of the power and work of the Holy Spirit, as often displayed through Pentecostal spirituality. Over the last twenty years, Pentecostal style churches in the Punjab have grown and multiplied dramatically. In November 2022, one of India's most prominent English-language magazines, *India Today*, ran a cover story called "Pastors of Punjab" profiling numerous mega-church and small village pastors. These churches, most of which have charismatic leaders and Pentecostal worship and spirituality, have become very large, some with gatherings in the multiple thousands. In addition, there has been a dramatic increase in the number of small churches throughout the region, with one estimate suggesting there could be as many as sixty-five thousand pastors across Punjab's twenty-three districts. The sizes of church may differ, but many of these share the Pentecostal emphases on prayer and miracles through spiritually powerful leaders. Sikhs from all castes and across the Punjab and elsewhere have been attracted and open to the supernatural displays of spiritual power.

This attraction to the supernatural in many ways reflects, as discussed above, the more devotional and mystical aspects of the Sikh tradition and some aspects of the *dera* culture and history of the region. Because of this it is not surprising that many Sikhs would be open to a mystical devotion that includes Jesus. As another personal example, I once had a conversation with an elderly Sikh woman who resided in California in the United States. At one point, as we discussed aspects of the Sikh and Christian faiths, she shared a story of how, one day, while praying in her house she had a vision of Jesus standing in front of her. In her vision Jesus looked at her in a warm and peaceful way, and then looked in the direction of the local Sikh gurdwara. There was no doubt in her mind that this was Jesus, and that he chose to appear to her and give her peace, even as a devoted Sikh. Spirituality, and even evangelism, that is open to and comfortable with supernatural visions, miracles and other experiences can resonate deeply with and be attractive to many Sikhs.

In conclusion, I have not sought to argue against Christian evangelism. The good news of Jesus is and can be exactly that—good news to Sikhs. Christians do, and should continue to seek ways to present a compelling vision of Jesus, and pray that Sikhs gain a desire to learn more and even follow Jesus. How do we do this? I will not seek to speak for other contexts other than my own in this, and suggest that perhaps we as Christians can begin by addressing the very real and historic barriers of fear and threat. Perhaps we can dismantle these by more intentionally collaborating with Sikhs on common causes, and become allies and even advocates for Sikhs. What might result if Christians actively seek the health of the Sikh community and advocate for them? How might trust be built if we showed interest in Sikhs and their gurdwaras, study the Sikh Scriptures with them, and learn about what they find meaningful about their faith? What if Christians sensitively experimented with ways to express a faith and devotion to Christ in ways that make sense to Sikhs?

We would hopefully do these things, not so we could eventually convert Sikhs to the Christian religion, reflecting a competitive religion paradigm. Rather, we would do this because the good news challenges the constructs of competitive religion. We would share our faith verbally and in action, but not coercively. And we would maintain our friendship and allyship no matter how our Sikh friends respond. We could and should offer to pray with and for them—even praying for God to do miracles in their lives. We could share meaningful Scriptures with them, even as we ask them to share with us Scriptures or prayers that are meaningful to them. We would also listen as our Sikh friends share with us, in whatever passionate and compelling ways, what they find meaningful in their own Sikh tradition. There should be space, in good relationships, for speech that seeks to persuade the other, and it should be mutual.

A common maxim in many discussions on evangelism says that people typically need to trust the messenger before they can trust the message.

And as we have seen, it can be difficult to build this quality between religious communities when one has used its greater power to coerce, control, and exploit the other. This is certainly at least one of the reasons why Christian evangelism has often created, or at least perpetuated, mistrust among Sikhs. Rebuilding that trust will not always be easy and will take time. And yet, we can hope and believe, trust can be rebuilt and Jesus can be more clearly seen. Perhaps if and when we start to acknowledge mistrust and its historical roots and respond by pursuing open, patient, and loving friendships, we can in some small ways help Sikhs see the gospel not as threatening news, but as the truly good news that it is.

Meaning of Evangelism in Relation to People of Other Faiths

It is crucial to recognize that religions are not static; they are dynamic movements that continually evolve. Contemporary Christianity in post-independence India differs significantly from the Christianity of the colonial era. Indian Christianity has become an integral part of India's religious ecology, shedding its foreign image. Christians have played pivotal roles in India's freedom movement and continue to be significant contributors to the country's educational and healthcare sectors. The Christian community's involvement in the non-profit sector is also substantial and cannot be overlooked.

Globally, Christianity promotes respectful engagement with people of other faiths, distancing itself from the contentious legacy of missionary activities during the colonial period. It is vital for Indian Christians to communicate this evolution to their Hindu and Sikh neighbors, highlighting the transformation from a historically foreign religion to a locally embedded faith that respects and enhances India's diverse cultural landscape.

Likewise, it is equally important to acknowledge the changes within Hindu and Sikh traditions in India. These religions have also undergone significant transformations, adapting to contemporary challenges and reflecting the dynamic nature of religious life. Recognizing these changes is essential for fostering mutual understanding and respect among different religious communities, facilitating a more inclusive and harmonious social environment.

Recognizing the complexity and diversity within each religious tradition is crucial for effective interfaith dialogue and evangelism. Hinduism, for example, can be likened to an ocean of traditions, each with its own distinct practices and beliefs. To effectively contextualize the gospel within such a diverse religious landscape, it is essential to understand these traditions on their own terms rather than simplifying them into a uniform entity or viewing them through a Christian-centric lens.

The conventional approach of studying world religions through textbooks is often inadequate for grasping the nuanced realities of these traditions. Instead, building relationships with faithful followers of other religions can provide deeper insights into the distinct nature of their beliefs and practices. This approach fosters a more authentic understanding and respects the integrity of each tradition.

Christians often prioritize scriptural studies and rational approaches when engaging with other religions, which can inadvertently downplay the rich, non-textual, and cultural traditions that form the backbone of many communities' religious experiences. For instance, both Hinduism and Sikhism have profound cultural dimensions that are integral to their religious practice and expression.

To effectively communicate the good news of Jesus Christ in a way that resonates with people from different religious backgrounds, it is essential to adopt a cultural approach. This means translating and presenting the gospel in the language and cultural forms familiar to those communities, thereby making it more accessible and relevant to their lived experiences. This approach not only enhances understanding but also builds bridges of mutual respect and cooperation among diverse religious groups.

Evangelism, often criticized for its predatory nature in India, must be re-envisioned to transcend mere proselytization. Recognizing the breadth of practices that constitute evangelism is crucial; it encompasses not only interfaith dialogue, preaching, and teaching but also extends to embodying friendship, hospitality, and discipleship. In a nation marked by profound economic disparities like India, evangelism must actively involve poverty alleviation, education, and the economic empowerment of the poor.

The Christian principle of the equality of all human beings holds special significance in a society deeply segmented by caste and sub-castes. Part of effective evangelism is therefore also women's empowerment, addressing and rectifying gender imbalances within these communities. Moreover, given India's secular framework, which champions a respect for diversity—be it religious, cultural, linguistic, or culinary—evangelism must adapt to preserve and respect these differences. The erosion of such diversity poses a significant threat, particularly in the current climate of rising religious nationalism.

Therefore, evangelism in India should not be a one-size-fits-all approach but should be tailored to meet the specific needs and sensibilities of each community and context. This means understanding and addressing the unique challenges and opportunities within different social and cultural settings, ensuring that evangelism is not only respectful and sensitive but also relevant and supportive of broader social development goals.

Bibliography

"Christian Conversion Event Cancelled after Sikh Complaints." Sikh Press Association, June 7, 2023. https://www.sikhpa.com/christiansikhconversioneventcancelled/.

Duerksen, Darren. *Ecclesial Identities in a Multi-Faith Context: Jesus Truth-Gatherings (Yeshu Satsangs) Among Hindus and Sikhs in Northwest India.* American Society of Missiology Monograph Series. Eugene, OR: Pickwick, 2015.

Fenech, Louis E. "The Evolution of the Sikh Community." *The Oxford Handbook of Sikh Studies*, edited by Pashaura Singh and Louis E. Fenech, 35–48. Oxford: Oxford University Press, 2014.

Gandhi, M. K. *In Search of the Supreme.* Vol. 3. Ahmedabad: Navajivan, 1961.

Humphrey, James Lorenzo. *Twenty-One Years in India.* Cincinnati: Jennings and Graham, 1905.

John, Vinod. *Believing Without Belonging? Religious Beliefs and Social Belonging of Hindu Devotees of Christ.* Eugene, OR: Pickwick, 2020.

Jones, E. Stanley. *The Christ of the Indian Road.* 1st ed. New York: Abingdon, 1925.

———. "Evangelism Among the Educated Indians." *Harvest Field* (1918) 289–96.

———. *Evangelize! Why? A Discussion of the Motives of Evangelism.* Nashville: Tidings, 1946.

Lobo, Lancy. "Visions and Illusions of Dalit Converts in India." *Social Action* 43 (1993) 439–53.

Martin, Paul Anthony John, "Missionary of the Indian Road: A Study of the Thought and Work of E. Stanley Jones between 1915 and 1948 in the Light of Certain Issues Raised by M. K. Gandhi for Anglo-Saxon Protestant Missionaries in India during the Period." PhD diss., University of Cambridge, 1988.

McLeod, W. H. "The Sikh Struggle in the Eighteenth Century and Its Relevance for Today." *History of Religions* 31 (1992) 344–62.

Oberoi, Harjot, ed. *The Construction of Religious Boundaries: Culture, Identity and Diversity in the Sikh Tradition.* Delhi: Oxford University Press, 1994.

Pickett, Jarrell Waskom. *Christian Mass Movements in India: A Study with Recommendations.* New York: Abingdon, 1933.

Singh, Harpreet. "'Western' Writers on the Sikhs." In *The Oxford Handbook of Sikh Studies*, edited by Pashaura Singh and Louis E. Fennech, 201–11. Oxford: Oxford University Press, 2014.

Chapter 8

Evangelism on Fire

Grassroots Evangelistic Modality of The Church of Pentecost from Ghana to the Nations

Christian Tsekpoe, David Nyansah Hayfron, Daniel Okyere Walker, Amos Jimmy Markin, and Rebecca Sey

Introduction

The growth of Pentecostal Christianity globally can be primarily attributed to its evangelistic zeal to reach the ends of the earth. Allan Anderson describes Pentecostalism as "fundamentally an 'end of the earth,' missionary, polycentric, transnational religion."[1] This growth in Pentecostalism is very visible in Africa, where Pentecostalism has been described as the representative face of Christianity on the continent.[2] The Church of Pentecost (CoP), a classical indigenous Pentecostal church in Ghana, has been identified as the fastest-growing Protestant church in Ghana. This growth is attributed to the church's intentional evangelistic drive and its emphasis on the practical manifestation of the gifts of the Holy Spirit.[3] This chapter explores the methodologies employed by the CoP to de-construct

1. Anderson, *To the Ends of the Earth*, 1.

2. Asamoah-Gyadu, "Pentecostalism and the Transformation of the African Christian Landscape."

3. Markin, *Transmitting the Spirit in Missions*.

traditional evangelistic strategies and to re-construct forms of evangelism that are consistent with biblical principles while maintaining cultural relevance in contemporary African contexts and other global regions. The chapter further examines grassroots evangelism initiatives launched in Ghana and other countries by the CoP, highlighting ongoing efforts to engage local communities on a global scale.

Models of Evangelism in the CoP

In the CoP, as has been the case in many African Pentecostal-Charismatic churches, the doctrine of the priesthood of all believers is actively practiced not only in worship and liturgy but also in evangelistic efforts.[4] All members of the church, irrespective of gender, age, educational or social status, are regarded as active participants in God's mission to reach the lost and the dying world for Christ. Such principles are practically exemplified through intentional evangelistic initiatives such as "All Ministries Rally"[5] and "One Member, One Discipled Soul" programs.[6] These efforts are based on the church's interpretation of relevant scriptural passages such as John 20:21, Matt 28:19, and Acts 1:8, as mandates for all believers, rather than for a select few. Consequently, each member of the church sees evangelism as a core aspect of their responsibility.

In his PhD thesis titled "The Pentecost Fire is Burning: Models of Mission Activities in The Church of Pentecost," Daniel Okyere Walker identifies five models of evangelism that have contributed to the church's growth.[7] The first model is the Local Mission Model, which encourages all church members, including new converts, to share their faith with family and friends within their local communities. Next is the Regional Mission Model, where church members who travel to neighboring African countries for any reason share their faith and establish churches. Similar to this model is the Migrational Mission Model, which describes the efforts of

4. Agyapong, "Priesthood of All Believers."

5. Specific dates are scheduled on the calendar of the CoP, where all the traditional ministries in the church, namely, men's ministry, women's ministry, youth ministry, evangelism ministry, and children's ministry, embark on intentional evangelism, including "open air campaigns."

6. An initiative where each member of the church is required to preach the gospel and bring at least one convert who will go through some level of discipleship in the church.

7. For details of these mission models, see Walker, "Pentecost Fire is Burning."

Ghanaian migrants in the Western and North American diaspora, who, through every available opportunity, evangelize and establish churches in countries where opportunities arise. Walker also identifies the Reverse Mission Model. This describes planned, organized efforts by the church's headquarters to preach the gospel and plant churches in Europe and North America. Lastly, Walker coins the Reflex Mission Model to describe how non-Ghanaian indigenous people engage with the CoP either in Ghana or elsewhere, return to their home countries to initiate the planting of CoP congregations. Typical examples of this model are the CoP in India and Pakistan.[8] These models practically demonstrate how each member of the church is expected to actively engage in evangelism.

Pneumatological Dimensions of Evangelism in the CoP

The role of the Holy Spirit in global mission in contemporary times has been discussed by many scholars.[9] Writing from an emic perspective, Amos Jimmy Markin has observed that, in carrying out the mission of God, the CoP not only embarks on Lamin Sanneh's idea of "translating the message" of the gospel in new contexts, but is also "transmitting the Spirit" from person to person and from context to context; the Holy Spirit Himself empowering, motivating and propelling church members to carry out mission activities.[10] Every new convert is encouraged to seek the baptism of the Holy Spirit. When a person is baptized in the Holy Spirit accompanied by the evidence of speaking in tongues, as happened in the book of Acts, he or she becomes transformed and empowered with spiritual gifts and great boldness.[11] Such persons are moved by the Holy Spirit to begin to share their conversion experiences and encounters with the Lord to their households, friends, communities, villages, and towns. Normally, because their regeneration and Spirit-baptism experiences lead to visible character and

8. Walker, "Pentecost Fire is Burning."

9. For instance, Kirsteen Kim discusses the Spirit's global work and how our local experiences of the Spirit can connect to that grand work. See Kim, *Joining in with the Spirit*, 1. Also, Amos Yong's "*missio-spiritus*" model for the third millennium shows how the action of the Spirit, right from the Old Testament until the eschatological New Jerusalem, helps us to focus on mission practices of Christian witness that embody worshipfulness, neighborliness, collaboration and forgiveness, and sojourn—being constantly on the move into new spaces. See Yong, *Mission After Pentecost*, 273–83.

10. Markin, *Transmitting the Spirit in Missions*, 288.

11. See Kärkkäinen, "Pentecostal Mission," 33–34.

lifestyle changes, their testimonies are believed by their hearers. In the CoP, evangelism is therefore done by all persons, from the new convert to the clergy. Without necessarily waiting for formal missions training, members of the CoP launch out under the power of the Holy Spirit to win souls and plant churches, and report their achievements to the leadership for further administrative actions.[12] CoP members typically expect the Holy Spirit to supply them with what to say, and also back their words with signs and wonders where necessary (Luke 12:12; 21:15; Mark 16:20).

Similar to what Yong describes as actions deployed by the early church, "as the Spirit gives utterance"[13] to minister to people of diverse backgrounds and conditions, the Holy Spirit inspires the CoP leadership to deploy various strategies for soul winning, including engaging persons from other faiths, the marginalized, persons with disability and those with deviant lifestyles in "languages" and ministry formats that would make sense to them.

For a church that started in sub-Saharan Africa to spread to over 190 nations of the world, one could only attribute such a staggering feat to the power and leadership of the Holy Spirit, who is the chief architect of its mission activities.

Eschatological Dimensions of Evangelism in the CoP

Pentecostals generally believe that the outpouring of the Holy Spirit "upon all people" as recorded in Acts 2:17 is an indication that the church is within the last days, a fulfillment of Joel's prophecy (Joel 2:28) that such a phenomenon will occur in the last days.[14] This eschatological understanding has motivated members of the CoP to preach the gospel with urgency and win souls, because "Jesus is coming soon." A careful observation of the CoP's contemporary evangelism methods reveals a revival of this eschatological fervency manifested in the introduction of new ministry interventions. Many of these new ministry interventions aim at reaching out to lost souls and bringing them to Christ. The expectation is for everyone to have the opportunity to hear the gospel before Jesus returns.[15]

12. Walker, "Pentecost Fire is Burning." 1–2.

13. Yong, *Missiological Spirit*, 37–54.

14. Ma, "Pentecostal Eschatology," 96.

15. For details of these ministry interventions, see The Church of Pentecost, *Vision 2028*.

Evangelism and Social Action in the CoP

Over the years, the CoP has endeavored to offer holistic ministry by keeping a good balance between soul-winning and church planting activities, and social action. The church has invested in education, health and other strategic social investments in partnership with governments and key development-focused organizations. The church has 104 basic schools, one vocational school, three senior high schools, and one university. The church also has four hospitals and eight clinics. Annually, huge sums of money are invested in the educational and health pursuits of church members.[16] The CoP has built several prisons in Ghana (to ease congestion) to support the efforts of the government.[17] In June 2025, the CoP built and handed over a fully functional, modern fire station to the Ghana Fire Service.[18] All these interventions have made CoP's mission more holistic and enhanced the outlook of the CoP as a progressive Pentecostal ministry.[19]

CoP Mission to the Nations

As earlier described, the spread of the CoP to many nations has been a collective effort of all members, including missionaries ordained and sent by the church's headquarters, individual travellers on their personal trips who carry the fire of the gospel in their bones, as well as students and young professionals who volunteer to serve in short-term missions under the umbrella of *PENSA International*.[20]

CoP missionaries have engaged in cross-cultural and cross-linguistic missions by being faithful to the Scriptures as well as adopting indigenous elements in worship such as music and dance, to enhance reception of the

16. For more details on the CoP's social actions, see Anim, "Pentecostal Mission and Social Transformation," 50–62.

17. For more on the social interventions of the CoP, see the Chairman's State of the Church address delivered at the 47th General Council Meetings held from April 30 to May 2, 2025, in Ghana.

18. For more details, visit Bonney, "Church of Pentecost."

19. See Daniels, "Progressive Pentecostalism, Pentecostal Philanthropy," 50–63.

20. *PENSA International* is a global body of tertiary students and alumni, serving as the missions force of The Church of Pentecost. It was launched by the chairman of The Church of Pentecost, apostle Eric Nyamekye, in May 2019. Their mandate is to break new grounds in the nations and establish PENSA groups in the nations which do not have an established students wing of the church.

gospel. Indigenous languages, food, and dresses are all adopted to make missionaries more appealing to new cultures they encounter.[21] In some nations where the CoP has been planted, one would observe that some elements of Ghanaian culture have been exported into those contexts, but the host culture is also being carefully destigmatized and integrated into their worship. In places where the Ghanaian culture dominated church life from its beginning, efforts are being made to relativize it, and allow for more indigenization, especially through its children, youth, and student ministries, in the hope that the indigenes will feel more "at home" in their own environment. Translating the message from Ghana to other contexts, just as Sanneh observed in the case of the spread of Christianity from its Jewish and Aramaic roots into gentile culture, must involve relativizing the home (sending) culture and destigmatization of the culture of the new contexts.[22]

The CoP strongly emphasizes the nineteenth-century Protestant mission ideas of Henry Venn and Rufus Anderson—self-supporting, self-governing, self-propagating—in its external missions.[23] As explained by David Bosch, these nineteenth century ideas were never formally abandoned, but were simply forgotten.[24] The early fathers of the CoP have re-dug these ideas from the nineteenth century to guide their mission work in contemporary times. Once indigenes or naturalized nationals accept Jesus Christ as their Lord and Savior, the mission strategy focuses on discipling and mentoring those who have leadership potential to take leadership responsibilities, and also raise resources from within their nations to support the work. Once a matured leadership team that can effectively govern the church is raised, leadership is usually handed over to these indigenous leaders to lead and mobilize a mission force within their nations to propagate the gospel to other parts of their nation and beyond.

21. Apostle Daniel and Rebecca Sey, for instance, who were called from Ghana to serve in Lusophone contexts, learned the Portuguese language as they worked in Cape Verde, Brazil, and Portugal, and also found effective ways of making friends with persons in these locations as a strategy to spread the work. Through them, The Church of Pentecost in these nations saw phenomenal growth and development.

22. Sanneh, *Translating the Message*, 12–15.

23. Bays, "Three-Self Patriotic Movement."

24. Bosch, *Transforming Mission*, 339, 460.

Contemporary Methods of Evangelism in the CoP—Practical Field Examples

As discussed earlier, members of the CoP are led by the Spirit to embark on evangelism in new locations. This is typical of the Pentecostal Movement, and done passionately by members whether as part of formalized church-organized outreaches, or on their personal travels in search for better life conditions.[25] Similar to the Acts 8:4–13 model, such efforts often lead to successful conversions, although not always.[26] Effective preparation in prayer and fasting before launching out to witness is, therefore, a key component of the strategy deployed by CoP members.

The Evangelism Ministry of The Church of Pentecost embraces all members of the church irrespective of gender, social class, or age. The children's ministry, youth, and PENSA[27] ministries have been very instrumental in winning and discipling new converts.

The CoP has effectively used the traditional evangelistic methods, such as personal evangelism, open-air crusades[28], rallies[29], sharing of tracts and visits to schools, beaches, markets, prisons and hospitals. The CoP has also adopted and adapted new methods of evangelism to remain relevant in a religiously and culturally pluralistic world. Some of these new ministry interventions include the Home and Urban Missions, which focuses on migrants, drug addicts, commercial sex workers, street dwellers, and other marginalized populations.[30] Another important initiative is the Ministry to Persons with Disabilities, which prioritizes the significance of salvation regardless of a person's disability. Other contemporary ministry interventions of the CoP include Ministry to Celebrities, the E-church, Schools

25. Anderson, *Introduction to Pentecostalism*, 206–7.

26. In Acts 8, whereas many people were genuinely converted to the faith, Simon the sorcerer's conversion remained questionable. Some persons encountered by CoP leaders and members in our outreaches have ended up bringing challenges to the church. See Pervo *Acts*.

27. PENSA is an acronym for "Pentecost Students and Associates." It is the student wing of the CoP and operates in tertiary and second-cycle institutions.

28. During open air crusades, large crowds are gathered on open fields, preferably in the evenings, where the gospel is communicated via public address systems to the masses. People are then invited to come forward to accept Jesus as Lord and Savior. It is often accompanied by praying for healing and deliverances.

29. Compared to crusades, rallies are smaller and may not need sophisticated PA systems.

30. Tsekpoe et al., "History and Growth."

Outreach Ministry, Chieftaincy Ministry, the Other Sheep Ministry (which focuses on persons of other faiths), Ministry to Markets, among others.

Conclusion

The CoP's grassroots evangelism exemplifies a dynamic, Spirit-empowered approach that actively involves all members in fulfilling the Great Commission. By integrating biblical principles with cultural relevance, utilizing diverse models, and emphasizing indigenization, the church has achieved remarkable growth both locally and globally. Its holistic mission strategy combines evangelism, social action, and indigenous cultural elements, making its outreach effective and sustainable in local and global contexts. This grassroots modality reveals the church's commitment to transforming lives through evangelism driven by the Holy Spirit, with an urgent eschatological outlook and a deep focus on community engagement.

Bibliography

Agyapong, Kwasi Atta. "The Priesthood of All Believers: Pentecostal–Charismatic Ecclesiology as the Nexus of Equipping" *E-Journal of Religious and Theological Studies* 11 (2025) 12–24.

Anderson, Allan. *An Introduction to Pentecostalism*. Cambridge: Cambridge University Press, 2004.

———. *To the Ends of the Earth: Pentecostalism and the Transformation of World Christianity*. Oxford: Oxford University Press, 2013.

Anim, Emmanuel Kwesi. "Pentecostal Mission and Social Transformation." In *Re-Visioning African Pentecostal-Charismatic Mission in the Public Sphere*, edited by Christian Tsekpoe and Lord Elorm-Donkor, 50–62. Eugene, OR: Pickwick, 2024.

Asamoah-Gyadu, Kwabena. "Pentecostalism and the Transformation of the African Christian Landscape." In *Pentecostalism in Africa: Presence and Impact of Pneumatic Christianity in Postcolonial Societies*, edited by Martin Lindhardt, 100–114. Leiden: Brill, 2015.

Bays, Daniel H. "Three-Self Patriotic Movement." In *The Encyclopedia of Christianity Online*, edited by John Mbiti. Leiden: Brill, 2016–2026. https://referenceworks.brill.com/display/entries/ECO/T.50.xml.

Bonney, Emmanuel. "Church of Pentecost Hands over Newly Built Fire Station to GNFS." Graphic Online, May 17, 2025. https://www.graphic.com.gh/news/general-news/ghana-news-church-of-pentecost-hands-over-newly-built-fire-station-to-gnfs.html.

Bosch, David J. *Transforming Mission: Paradigm Shifts in Theology of Mission*. Twentieth Anniversary ed. American Society of Missiology Series, No. 16. Maryknoll, NY: Orbis, 2011.

The Church of Pentecost. *Vision 2028: Five-Year Vision Document for the Church of Pentecost Covering the Period 2023–2028*. https://thecophq.org/wp-content/uploads/2024/07/The-COP-Vision-2024-2028.pdf.

Daniels, David. "Progressive Pentecostalism, Pentecostal Philanthropy: The Church of Pentecost." In *African Pentecostal Missions Maturing: Essays in Honor of Aps Opoku Onyinah*, edited by Lord Elorm-Donkor and Clifton Clarke, 50–63. Eugene, OR: Pickwick, 2018.

Kärkkäinen, Veli-Matti. "Pentecostal Mission: A Theological Appraisal." In *African Pentecostal Missions Maturing: Essays in Honor of Aps Opoku Onyinah*, edited by Lord Elorm-Donkor and Clifton Clarke, 33–34. Eugene, OR: Pickwick, 2018.

Kim, Kirsteen. *Joining in with the Spirit: Connecting World Church and Local Mission*. London: SCM, 2012.

Ma, Wonsuk. "Pentecostal Eschatology: What Happened When the Wave Hit the West End of the Ocean." *Asian Journal of Pentecostal Studies* 12 (2009), 96.

Markin, Amos J. *Transmitting the Spirit in Missions: The History and Growth of the Church of Pentecost*. Eugene, OR: Wipf & Stock, 2019.

Pervo, Richard I. *Acts: A Commentary*. Edited by Harold W. Attridge. Hermeneia—A Critical and Historical Commentary on the Bible. Minneapolis: Fortress, 2009.

Sanneh, Lamin O. *Translating the Message: The Missionary Impact on Culture*. 2nd ed., rev. and exp. American Society of Missiology Series. Maryknoll, NY: Orbis, 2009.

Tsekpoe, Christian, et al. "The History and Growth of the Home and Urban Mission of the Church of Pentecost, Ghana." *Pentecostalism, Charismatism and Neo-Prophetic Movements Journal* 5 (2024) 45–68.

Walker, Daniel Okyere. "The Pentecost Fire is Burning: Models of Mission Activities in the Church of Pentecost." PhD thesis, University of Birmingham, 2010.

Yong, Amos. *The Missiological Spirit: Christian Mission Theology in the Third Millennium Global Context*. Eugene, OR: Cascade, 2014.

———. *Mission After Pentecost: The Witness of the Spirit from Genesis to Revelation*. Grand Rapids: Baker Academic, 2019.

Chapter 9

Communal Evangelism from the Margins

Alexia Salvatierra and Brandon Wrencher

Introduction

How do we come to know Jesus? Many Evangelicals would answer that an individual hears the good news of Jesus' death and resurrection—God's saving act from sin, death, and the devil—and then responds personally to the invitation to follow him. Yet in the two movements we explore here, people encountered Jesus not as isolated individuals but through his Body—the gathered witness of believers incarnating his Spirit in the world.

The historical and risen Christ is not absent in such encounters; rather, he is mediated through particular human communities. In this chapter, we describe and analyze two such movements: the Base Christian Community movements in Latin America and the Philippines during the 1970s and 1980s, and the Hush Harbors—the independent churches of enslaved Africans in the antebellum South.

These communities share more than simple Christian faith. Their membership and leadership arose largely from among the oppressed and marginalized. Within them, believers experienced Jesus and the Holy Spirit as sources of healing and liberation in both personal and communal life. Collectively, these communities became forces for social transformation and justice. Their discipleship was holistic and missional, moving society toward the will of God.

From our study of these two movements, we identified five shared principles that may guide the formation of similar communities in the twenty-first century. Today, in the global North and West, the church faces a profound crisis of faith—visible in the accelerating exodus of younger generations. We believe that communities embodying the holistic life of Christ can become spaces where those who have rejected traditional forms of church might yet come to know, love, and follow Jesus. Before turning to the five common principles, we first share the personal and contextual experiences that led each of us to this study.

Alexia

I belonged to one of the first churches to officially join the Sanctuary Movement for Central American refugees in 1980. Through that movement, I encountered base Christian communities in El Salvador and Guatemala and was profoundly shaped by them. Later, from 1984 to 1987, I served as a missionary in the Philippines, participating in the pro-democracy movement against the Marcos dictatorship, where again I was part of a base Christian community.

Over the years, young people—primarily young Latino/a/x leaders—have shared with me their visions for the kind of church they long to build. Each time they describe their dream, memories of those base Christian communities return vividly. In them, I had seen precisely the kind of church these young leaders imagine.

I felt a strong calling to make that experience available to new generations. As both practitioner and scholar, I sought to study the movement not merely through personal recollection but through disciplined research—reading sources, conducting interviews, and examining the historical record—so that this remarkable witness could inspire those renewing the church today.

Brandon

I am an ordained pastor in the United Methodist Church. Several years ago, my bishop and district superintendent in North Carolina asked me to plant a multiracial faith community near downtown Greensboro—one centered on mission and justice.

To prepare, I was required to find a mentor and to join a learning cohort. Yet most of the available models did not resonate with my cultural or theological heritage. Seeking guidance, I reached out to Alexia, saying, "I'm struggling to find examples that reflect my commitment to Jesus' ministry in the world and to a communal, justice-oriented way of being the church."

Our conversations deepened. I was also in dialogue with colleagues experimenting with new ecclesial forms—many of us clergy-activists seeking a faith community that embodied both the gospel and social transformation. Together, we began studying Base Ecclesial Communities and Hush Harbors.

When the Holy Spirit stirs deep hunger and longing, and trusted mentors journey beside you, bold acts of faithful experimentation often follow. Eventually, I planted a community called Good Neighbor Movement in Greensboro, continuing under Alexia's mentorship. Through those years of collaboration, she proposed that we write together—placing these two historic movements in conversation. The book *Buried Seeds* and this chapter are the fruit of that shared labor.

The History of the Base Christian Community Movement

The Base Christian Community (BCC) movement emerged after the Second Vatican Council of the Roman Catholic Church (1962–1965). Rooted in the Council's 1966 document *Gaudium et Spes*, which defined the church as *alma y fermenta de la comunidad*—"the soul and the yeast of the community"—the BCC movement reimagined ecclesial life from the ground up.

These small, neighborhood-based communities—initially simple Bible study groups—flourished in Latin America, the Philippines, and later in parts of Africa. Composed primarily of poor and marginalized believers, they became vibrant, holistic expressions of the body of Christ and the spiritual backbone of movements for peace and justice.

I personally witnessed the 1987 EDSA People Power Revolution in the Philippines, when more than a million citizens nonviolently deposed the Marcos dictatorship. The BCCs played a central role in sustaining the spiritual and moral energy of that historic struggle.

Brandon

The Hush Harbor movement arose in the antebellum South among enslaved Africans. These secret gatherings—sometimes called the Invisible

Institution—were spaces where enslaved people met to worship, pray, and study Scripture beyond the surveillance of the plantation system.

Scholars have long debated whether Christianity was merely "the religion of the oppressor." The Hush Harbors offer a powerful counter-witness. Enslaved Africans, though introduced to Christianity through violent coercion, were profoundly moved by its stories—especially the Exodus, the life of Jesus, and the power of the Holy Spirit. They interpreted these through the lens of their African spiritual heritage, discovering in them a God of liberation.

Defying prohibitions and risking their lives, they stole away into the woods to meet, sing, preach, and strategize. In those hidden places, they experienced freedom in the Spirit and envisioned God's kingdom breaking into their present reality. The Hush Harbors became the spiritual seedbed of later social and political movements for freedom.

The Five Common Principles Shared by the BCCs and the Hush Harbors

From our comparative study, we identified five shared principles that define both movements:

1. Familia / Kinship
2. Participación / Leaderfull
3. Conscientización / Woke
4. Spirit-uality
5. Faith-full Organizing

We explore each principle through stories of lived experience, inviting readers to reflect on their own communities—celebrating parallels and confronting challenges toward deeper and more holistic discipleship.

Familia / Kinship

Every faithful Christian gathering carries a sense of family. Yet these movements elevated *familia* to a transformative level. In the BCC movement, belonging often meant risking one's life. During the civil wars in the Philippines and El Salvador, simply carrying a Bible could mark someone as a catechist and lead to disappearance or death. Members pledged to adopt one another's children if parents were taken. *That* is *familia*.

This commitment extended beyond regular participants. One evening, when a poor family attended a Bible study for the first time, the leaders announced that the next gathering would be at their house. Ashamed, the newcomers protested, "You can't come to our house—there are holes in the roof." The leaders replied, "The study is on Friday. We'll come Tuesday to fix your roof, and see you Friday."

Familia also reached beyond local borders. When famine struck Nicaragua, a BCC in El Salvador collected aid. A farm laborer placed his only bag of beans—the day's meal—on the altar for Nicaraguan brothers and sisters. He turned to leave, then came back, removed his sole coat, and laid it beside the beans. That too is *familia*.

In West African religious traditions, women were often regarded as the sacred center of community and the primary mediators of divine presence—the *sacred feminine*. Within the Hush Harbors, enslaved Africans retrieved this sensibility. They recognized that the path to healing and liberation often began with the leadership of Black women.

Despite families being torn apart by the slave system, enslaved people forged kinship through shared spiritual life. One of their primary practices of connection was singing. The *Negro Spirituals*—born directly out of the Hush Harbor experience—became a theology in song, expressing grief, resistance, and eschatological hope.

Though most could not read or write, they interpreted Scripture through these songs, embodying theology through rhythm and voice. Singing united them across plantations and generations, creating spiritual kinship that defied bondage and prefigured freedom.

The other aspect of kinship that was crucial for the Hush Harbors is that they created kinship in a way that helped enslaved Africans experience safety, even when so much of their lives was controlled. As I shared earlier, their lives were constantly under surveillance and marked by brutality. Yet the Hush Harbors provided a counterworld—a sanctuary of belonging and trust.

They knew these spaces needed to be small enough for people to truly know one another. On the plantation, life was measured by production and output, not humanity or the *Imago Dei*. In contrast, Hush Harbors were intentionally intimate gatherings where one's personhood was recognized.

They were also safe in another sense. Whereas plantation Christianity often assimilated to the political status quo—justifying slavery as acceptable in God's eyes—the Hush Harbors required commitment and discernment. To belong, one had to be vetted. There was a genuine sense of discipleship and risk, a recognition that joining meant breaking rank with the status quo.

In many contemporary churches, we often see signs outside declaring, "All are welcome." That inclusive spirit certainly resonated in the Hush Harbors, but there was also clarity: if you were going to be part of what God was doing in that community, you had to *count the cost.* Which Jesus were you talking about?

I think about this in relation to my own experience (Brandon) of trying to pattern our faith community, the Good Neighbor Movement, after the Hush Harbors—embodying this same sense of kinship. We organized ourselves into what we called City Villages. These were our small groups, patterned after both the Hush Harbors and the basic ecclesial communities.

One City Village, in particular, was led by women—women of color. The woman who helped us start it was a business owner who ran a coffee shop in the neighborhood. Because of the pressures of gentrification, she eventually had to close her shop. As they prepared to transition out of that space, the women invited me—even though it was a women-only group—to join them in a closing ritual.

They brought a small cast iron pot and invited everyone to write down memories of where God had shown up in their lives and in their City Village. Each person placed their note into the pot, and the memories were burned as an act of offering. I went last, aware that this was not my space, but grateful to be welcomed into it. As I stepped forward, I unexpectedly began to weep and felt embarrassed. One of the women placed her hand on my shoulder and said, "No, Brandon. It's okay. Your tears are welcome here. That's what we do."

That moment captured the essence of kinship—a faith community creating safety even among those who did not share biological ties, but who shared a commitment to following Jesus and living by the Spirit. It was, in its own way, a contemporary hush harbor—an embodiment of sacred safety, kinship, and Spirit-led belonging.

Participación / Leaderfull

In the base Christian communities (BCCs), almost no one would have been recognized as a leader in the broader society. Yet they believed they were the Body of Christ and that every member was essential. They took 1 Cor 12:24 seriously: those who had received less honor must be intentionally honored. In today's terms, those who were marginalized had to be centered.

They lived this conviction in tangible ways. Each community trained multiple people for leadership. Two roles existed in every gathering: the *coordinator* (*coordinador* or *coordinadora*), and the *animador* or *animadora*—a person attentive to the spiritual atmosphere of the group. The *animador/a* sought to inspire and ensure that the community remained responsive to the Spirit, while the coordinator guided the meeting toward its shared objectives.

They also took seriously that every gift was part of one's mission. Every skill—manual, intellectual, or relational—was considered a contribution to the life of the body. For instance, Nacho, a skilled bricklayer known for his drinking, womanizing, and abuse of his wife, was not initially part of the BCC. Yet the community needed his craft to build a new school. They approached him, saying, "We believe God has called you to lay the bricks for this school. You are God's agent in this work." Nacho agreed. Later, he said there had been a war within him—between the alcohol and the school—and *the school won.* Through that act of service, he became a committed member of the community and a follower of Jesus.

This sense that being *leaderfull* meant an intentional reversal of societal expectations about who could lead and what leadership meant. "Everybody is somebody." That phrase still lives on in Black communities today.

In the Hush Harbors, leadership was not centered on a single, recognizable figure. In contemporary churches, we often identify our community by its pastor—"My pastor is Reverend Doctor so-and-so." There is nothing wrong with that, but the Hush Harbors were different. Their pastors were largely unknown. You would not have identified these sacred spaces by a senior pastor or charismatic figure.

These were risky spaces—communities living out the gospel in ways that defied the status quo. To put one leader in front would endanger not only the individual but the entire community and its mission. Therefore, leadership was shared. Every idea, even risky ones, was considered part of discerning how God was moving among them.

Rachel Harding writes in *Remnants* about her grandmother, a formerly enslaved woman connected to the Hush Harbors. When asked whether she knew of Harriet Tubman, her grandmother responded, "Which Harriet?"—implying there were many Harriets. That testimony reflects how leadership was understood: not as singular heroism but as collective discipleship.

The Hush Harbors modeled decision-making that was communal, not corporate. It did not always mean consensus, but it required deep trust that the Spirit was moving among everyone. I think of an example from my own community in Winston-Salem, North Carolina, when we launched a campaign to address gun violence in a working-class Black neighborhood.

We invited the entire community to discern together what issue to pursue. Ultimately, the decision that emerged wasn't the one we, as organizers, had envisioned. One brother named Pres (short for President) challenged us, saying, "Don't babysit me. Don't treat us like dummies. If we decide this is what God is calling us to, and we fail, let us learn from our own mistakes and grow." That moment was transformative. It reminded us that the Spirit speaks through everyone—that even failure can be a site of grace and growth.

Conscientización / Woke

We've been talking about the collapsing boundary between leader and follower. But the base Christian communities also broke down the boundary between church and world. For them, the entire world was God's world; Jesus was Lord of the universe.

This conviction transformed how they understood their struggles. Problems were no longer seen as merely personal but as interconnected with social and structural realities. When a child struggled in school, parents stopped saying, "My child is a burro; he's stupid," and instead asked, "Why is my child struggling? Is it my child, the school, or both? And why is the school this way?" They kept asking "Why?" until they saw how the personal and social intertwined.

This process—*conscientización*—was developed by Paulo Freire. But the BCCs went further. They recognized that liberation required more than social analysis; it demanded spiritual truth. They knew that casting out falsehoods without filling the void with divine truth only left room for new oppressions.

When oppressed people examined the lies told about them, they recognized unholy intentions behind those narratives. The question then became: *What is the divine truth?* The divine truth was that God made their children, and God called them to be agents in the world.

Mary's *Magnificat* was beloved in the BCCs because Mary, whom the world deemed insignificant, was chosen to change history. The Word of God became their story. Each Bible study followed the *reflection-action cycle*—learning, acting, and reflecting again—believing that true understanding of God's will comes only through obedience.

They understood that revelation unfolds through practice: as we live into God's will, God reveals more of it to us. Their reflection-action process was not merely sociological; it was profoundly theological—a participation in the divine-human relationship.

For enslaved Africans in the Hush Harbors, reflection and action looked different. Most were illiterate, so learning occurred primarily through oral tradition. Their theology was *encrypted*—coded within the language, songs, and stories they heard.

Through these oral and symbolic forms, they discerned divine truth for themselves, reclaiming their identity as *children of God*, not property of another. This is why I'm intentional about using the term *enslaved people* rather than *slaves*—language matters.

Within the Hush Harbors, theology was not read but sung, not written but lived. Through spirituals and coded speech, they translated the imposed theology of the plantation into a liberating gospel—one that proclaimed freedom, dignity, and God's presence with the oppressed.

I want to offer some examples of how the language of the enslaved functioned as a kind of gospel—songs that were both spirituals and codes of resistance. One such song is *Steal Away.* Many of you may know it, but few realize how subversive it truly was. On the surface, it appeared to those within the plantation system—those preaching an "oppressor's gospel," a domesticated religion—that the song's refrain, "Steal away to Jesus," referred merely to a heavenly hope. They believed the enslaved were accepting their suffering on earth and waiting for liberation in heaven.

In reality, these words were coded language for "stealing a meeting." When the community sang *Steal Away*, it signaled that a secret gathering would take place that night—often deep in the woods—where they would worship God freely and plan for their own liberation. These songs were not about resignation but about reflection and action, a theology formed apart from the indoctrination of the plantation church.

Another example is the spiritual *Everybody Talkin' 'Bout Heaven.* It is often misunderstood as a song about personal morality or spiritual purity. Yet its deeper message was prophetic: it condemned the hypocrisy of slaveholders who tried to wed chattel slavery to Christianity. The song warned that divine judgment would come upon a church that distorted the gospel to uphold oppression.

In the Hush Harbors, enslaved Africans embodied a theology of consciousness—a spirituality that refused to remain abstract or intellectual. Knowledge was carried not only in the mind but in the body. This *soma*—the fullness of flesh, emotion, and creation—became a vessel of divine knowing. The natural world itself joined in this divine conversation: bent twigs, the rush of water, or the beat of the drum all became sacred signals calling the faithful to gather, to worship, and to organize.

Even *Wade in the Water*, often mistaken for a baptismal hymn, was a call to escape—guiding fugitives to walk through water to evade the scent of the hounds. These were not merely songs of comfort; they were acts of embodied theology—where faith, knowledge, and liberation were sung, moved, and lived.

Spirituality

Traditional Evangelicals often question whether attention to social justice weakens spirituality. That was not the experience of either the Base Christian Communities (BCCs) or the Hush Harbors.

Ana, a leader in the BCC for over twenty years, recalled joining as a college student. She traveled from her campus to a poor, marginalized community, risking danger and inconvenience, because she found joy there—the profound joy of the Spirit present in small homes of study and worship. It was a joy rooted both in ecstatic worship, so characteristic of Latino/a spirituality, and in the tangible hope that "our children will eat." The union of these two joys—the joy of the Spirit and the joy of justice—was the hallmark of a Holy Spirit–filled spirituality.

This Spirit-grounded life emphasized not only joy but also hope and reconciliation. The BCCs believed in the hope of the resurrection so deeply that when members were "disappeared" by death squads, the community held rituals where they named the lost aloud, to which all would respond, *presente*—"present in the room."

They also practiced reconciliation courageously. When someone betrayed the community—whether from fear or greed—they sought to restore them to fellowship, saying, "Our lives are hidden in Christ. If we die, we die." Many did die, yet the community thrived. As Tertullian observed, "The blood of the martyrs is the seed of the church." Not all were fearless; some fled to the United States or other countries. Yet those who remained bore witness that love and faith could not be silenced.

What spirituality looked like in the Hush Harbors was deeply embodied. Singing, for instance, was an act of bodily worship—especially under the constant threat of surveillance. Worship had to be physical because it was an act of resistance, a declaration of freedom under watchful eyes.

Perhaps the most vivid example is found in Toni Morrison's *Beloved*. There, Baby Suggs—an enslaved woman and preacher—gathers her people in the clearing: men, women, children, elders. She calls them to embodied worship in what became known as the *ring shout*, an early expression of African American spirituality still alive in Pentecostal and Charismatic churches today.

She says, "Children, laugh," and they laugh. "Women, weep," and they wail for the sorrows of injustice. "Men, dance," and they move in circles, living the joy of freedom not yet visible but already promised. This was not abstract worship but worship that moved through the body, allowing lament, courage, and joy to rise together. It was faith that God was animating their very flesh to resist despair and to work for liberation.

Faith-Full Organizing

The final principle is *faith-full organizing*. The BCCs did not separate church and world. All of it belonged to God. Nor did they divide direct service, community development, and organizing for justice—they saw these as one continuous act of discipleship.

When invited into social transformation, their question was not "Is this faithful?" but "Why not?" Everything was done unto the Lord, including organizing. One BCC community, denied access to clean water, went to the mayor to demand running water. The mayor mocked them: "You poor people couldn't have thought of this yourselves. Who told you to come to me?" They looked at one another, then replied simply, "Jesus."

Faith-full organizing was not optional. It was not the work of a few "activists" but of the whole gospel community. Everyone was responsible for justice and peace in their local context, even while allowing diversity of political affiliation and method.

I want to return to the diversity of ways people join in God's liberating work. Think of Nat Turner, Gabriel Prosser, Harriet Tubman, and Frederick Douglass—leaders of social movements rooted in their faith. Douglass, for instance, spoke of "the Christianity of Christ" versus "the Christianity of this land." Where did he learn to draw such a distinction? Certainly not in the plantation church. He learned it in the Hush Harbors—those underground sanctuaries where enslaved Africans were free to interpret Scripture as a weapon of hope and resistance.

In those gatherings, the gospel was not an instrument of submission but an *animating presence*. It empowered them to say, "Chattel slavery is not God's will. God desires freedom, not just for us, but for all." That was faithful organizing in the Hush Harbors—a theology lived, sung, and embodied.

The Twenty-First-Century Application

In places like El Salvador, the BCCs continue today, often led by the grandchildren of their founders. Their ties to the Catholic Church have loosened, and their ecumenical partnerships have grown. Many communities now place a cup of water on the altar as a symbol of global thirst—both physical and spiritual—as access to clean water remains a pressing injustice.

In the United States, however, forming BCC- or hush harbor–style communities is more complex. Individualism, social isolation, and the varied layers of privilege and oppression pose real challenges. In East Los Angeles during the 1980s, a BCC emerged among refugees at Dolores Mission. That community birthed many vital ministries, including Homeboy Industries. Yet as members invested more in programs than in communal life, the BCC itself faded. Translating these principles to the US context is not simple.

In our book, *Buried Seeds: Learning from the Vibrant Resiliency of Marginalized Christian Communities*, we write to three audiences—Lydia, Amos, and Ruth. *Amos* represents the poor and marginalized. *Lydia* represents the privileged. *Ruth* represents those who have lived in both worlds. Our conviction is that Lydias and Ruths cannot live out these principles without Amos in leadership. God lifts up the poor for the sake of the whole.

This requires trusting voices society distrusts. During the height of the BCC movement, some theologians feared that the untrained poor would stray theologically. One woman responded to a priest's concern with profound clarity: "Father, it's not the parts of Scripture we don't understand that are hard. It's the parts we do understand that are hard to live—but when we live them, we understand."

Conclusion

In spite of every challenge, we believe God still calls the church to faithful witness—to be the living Body of Christ in the world. We stand amid a great cloud of witnesses. May we draw strength from their courage, wisdom from their example, and transformation through their faithfulness.

In contemporary liberation theology—particularly within the lineage of the Black church and Black liberation theology—we often speak of a *hermeneutic of suspicion.* In my book, I draw upon that language but also seek to challenge the idea that suspicion is the core of the hermeneutic. Within the hush harbors, and certainly within the faith community I helped to plant, which sought to model itself after those early ecclesial communities, there was far more than suspicion at work. There was a profound sense of *creativity at play*—a deep effort to listen not only to the plain meaning of the text and what was happening in the world but also to discern what God might be saying to us. This listening was not only for personal edification but for discerning how we might act faithfully amid the forces and injustices that shape our world.

In 2018, an unarmed Black man named Marcus Dion Smith was killed by the Greensboro Police Department while experiencing a mental health crisis during a downtown festival. Around that same time, our small hush harbor—one of our city villages—was gathered, reading Mary's *Magnificat.* As we read together, one member observed how familiar the passage felt in light of Marcus's death. Marcus had cried out for help, for recognition of his humanity, but the institutions of our city—the police, the hospital, and the broader social systems—essentially told him there was no room for him.

In that moment, we could not remain in an intellectual space. We sensed that God was calling us to respond to this sacred connection between Scripture and the present. In Mary's song, we hear a proclamation of divine reversal—of God setting things right even amid profound injustice. So, we organized a vigil with Marcus's family and the broader community, gathering people across racial and cultural lines—Latinx, Black, and white neighbors alike.

During that vigil, we enacted a contemporary Las Posadas—a tradition Alexia can describe more powerfully than I can. At its heart, *Las Posadas* reenacts the holy family's search for shelter, dramatizing rejection by institutions and offering a prophetic vision of radical hospitality. In our context, Marcus embodied that rejection. The police, called to protect and serve, said no. Religious institutions, called to be healers, said no. Yet the gospel reminds us that they do not have the final word. The power of Mary's *Magnificat*—and of our witness that night—was the proclamation that God's justice and love still prevail. God says, "Marcus is welcome," and so are we all.

That, to me, is the message of the hush harbor tradition: that we are called to build communities and institutions where all of God's people are truly welcomed. So, I want to leave you with this conviction—so much more is possible than we believe is possible.

Chapter 10

Church Plants as Evangelism Laboratories[1]

Len Tang

Introduction

As I was preparing to plant my first church outside of Portland, Oregon, I sought the guidance of a local pastor whose church was experiencing such tremendous conversion growth that it was spontaneously planting new churches in the area. The primary metaphor his church used as its inspiration was Lifeboat 14, taken from the story of the Titanic. In fact, in the lobby of the church building was a full-size replica of Lifeboat 14. The true story goes that as the Titanic sank on her maiden voyage and people were drowning in the ice-cold water, nearly all the lifeboats rowed away from those struggling in the water for fear of being swamped by survivors. Lifeboat 14, under the command of officer Harold Lowe, was the only lifeboat that rowed back and ultimately saved five people from drowning. The pastor posed the question, "Is the church a leisure ship dedicated to the comfort of its passengers or a lifeboat devoted to rescuing lost people?"

Church planters on the whole are dedicated to launching as many lifeboats as possible. Evangelism is one of the fundamental purposes of church planting and one of the primary motivations of church planters, including myself. One of the most oft-quoted rationales for church planting came

1. A longer version of this article appeared in *Fuller Magazine*: Tang, "Church Plants as Evangelism Laboratories."

back in 1990 from Fuller's own Peter Wagner in his book *Church Planting for a Greater Harvest*: "The single most effective evangelistic methodology under heaven is planting new churches."[2] (I just heard a planter use this quote in a podcast from April 2023). Again in 2002, the late Tim Keller reaffirmed this line of thinking in his article "Why Plant Churches?," writing that "the vigorous, continual planting of new congregations is the single most crucial strategy for (1) the numerical growth of the body of Christ in a city and (2) the continual corporate renewal and revival of the existing churches in a city."[3]

Broadly speaking, both personal experience and studies show that new churches are far more effective at winning people to Christ than established churches. For instance, in the Southern Baptist Convention (the largest church planting organization in the US, planting between six hundred and eight hundred churches per year), a 2018 report showed that church plants baptize more people per attendee than established churches—a 67 percent better attendee-to-baptism ratio.[4]

Whether or not church planting is the "most effective" or "most crucial" strategy for evangelism, this article will argue that it has been and will remain an absolutely essential element of the church's evangelistic witness in the world. Church planting often functions as the "R&D wing" of the church because of how much pioneering missional and evangelistic experimentation takes place through church plants as they engage in new and creative forms of engaging a diverse and disruptive culture with the gospel. Church planters and their teams are often a combination of entrepreneurial and evangelistic. The "research and development" that church plants discern and discover are then meant to flow back into the wider body of Christ to help the church engage and impact the culture with the gospel more broadly—hence Keller's second point that planting contributes to "the corporate renewal and revival of the existing churches in a city."

It's important to note that this article primarily reflects the mainstream North American church planting world, which is typically white and Protestant. There are many churches planted by and for Blacks, Latinos, and Asians in the United States, and one of the realities is that many of those churches fly under the radar because they function quite autonomously, are often small, and are not necessarily part of established denominational

2. Wagner, *Church Planting for a Greater Harvest*, 11.

3. Keller, "Why Plant Churches?"

4. Bingham, "NAMB SBC Report."

structures that track and report results. In addition, global Christianity has clearly shifted to the global South and so I am also not speaking to the thousands of churches planted by global Christians.

Why Are Church Plants More Evangelistic than Established Churches?

It is helpful to identify why church plants are generally more effective in reaching people for Christ than established churches. In his 2019 book *You Found Me* on congregational practices of evangelism, Rick Richardson surveyed and researched forty-five hundred North American churches. He identified that 10 percent of churches are experiencing conversion growth (as opposed to transfer growth). He calls these congregations "conversion communities" and identifies three common characteristics: missional imagination, missional leadership, and missional congregational practices.[5] It's no coincidence these characteristics are precisely what healthy church plants are designed to cultivate.

1. Church Planters Are Motivated by a Missional Imagination

Richardson describes recovering a missional imagination as becoming reenchanted by the power and beauty of the mission of Jesus, as well as recapturing a vision for the church as salt and light in the world. The vast majority of church planters I meet have a strong sense of "holy discontent," believing that an absolutely crucial aspect of the gospel of Jesus Christ is missing in the church. They feel indignant that a dimension of Christ's mission in the world is absent from people's lives and it breaks their heart. And they believe that a fresh expression of the body of Christ can reach people for Christ that existing churches cannot.

2. Church Planters Are Selected and Trained for Mission

Church planting networks and denominations actively seek out missional leaders with apostolic and evangelistic gifts to start new churches. Alan Hirsch has popularized the framing of the leadership gifts from Eph 4 as "APEST," an acronym for apostles, prophets, evangelists, shepherds, and

5. Richardson, *You Found Me*.

teachers. Church planting movements intentionally recruit "APEs"—leaders with apostolic, prophetic, and/or evangelistic gifts. Church planting organizations often host formal multi-day church planter assessments, designed to vet and "greenlight" APEs to start new churches. And church planters are typically trained to do neighborhood exegesis, and learn how to articulate and embody the gospel in their specific context. All these intentional processes tend to identify leaders who are gifted and burdened to share the gospel and lead people to Christ.

Pastors of established churches don't generally receive the same level of vetting and training as church planters, and established churches tend to prefer and affirm the classic pastoral gifts of STs (shepherds and teachers). During the pandemic, anecdotally it seems that pastors with ST gifts struggled even more since they were forced to become televangelists (due to live-streaming their sermons) as well as church planters (due to the need to freshly engage their physical and online communities).

3. Church Plants Function as "Conversion Communities"

Church plants have a higher likelihood of becoming conversion communities because the church plant is birthed into existence out of a desire to impact their community with the gospel. Church planters are prayerful and intentional in selecting leaders who share the church's evangelistic DNA. Church planting teams often seek to live as a missionary community in which they fan out across a city to identify groups receptive to the gospel (the "missionary" part) and then seek to live and love one another such that they are embodying a countercultural and communal way of life (the "community" part).

By contrast, it's often difficult for established churches to reach beyond meeting the needs of the already-converted. (Though it must be noted that every church plant eventually becomes an established church and must inevitably fight the same gravitational pull of focusing primarily or even exclusively on serving current members).

Dysfunctional Planting Narratives

Unfortunately, the same evangelistic zeal that drives church planting organizations often leads to theological errors or methodological excesses. The shadow side of church planters is that the very things that drive those leaders are the same things that can breed excess and exploitation. This is why the Fuller Church Planting Initiative (FCPI), which I lead, puts a huge emphasis on the spiritual formation of the planter and their team. Here are some of the dysfunctional narratives arising in church plants:

1. Theological Issue: Triumphalism

Often the language and imagery used in the mainstream church planting world is militaristic ("parachuting in," "taking a city for Christ") and triumphalistic. While the metaphors of multiplication and reproduction are certainly biblical (the seed growing on good soil multiplies thirty, sixty, or one hundred times), it is balanced by the need for the seed to first die in order to bear fruit, and the reality that the downward way of Jesus ultimately leads to the cross.

2. Racial Issue: Colonialism

Much of the mainstream church planting world still operates on what Toby Kurth calls "the white success story model" where the primary narrative has been that of a white, male, wealthy, suburban church planter who raises insane amounts of money to plant a large and growing attractional church.

3. Economic Issue: Gentrification

A further implication of a colonial approach is that planters who are unaware of their social location or neighborhood dynamics can unwittingly contribute to gentrification.

4. Psychological Issue: Narcissism and Celebrity Pastor Culture

The recent fall of many prominent church planters has highlighted the reality that church planting attracts and even affirms narcissistic leaders, and creates systems in which abuse of power is rampant because no accountability structures exist within highly autonomous church plants.

New Models of Holistic Evangelism

Even given the dangers inherent in church planting, by definition it is a crucible in which de-construction must ultimately give way to re-construction. So what might be some of the new narratives, models, and practices that church planting can offer in proclaiming the good news of Jesus afresh to the next generation?

1. New Narratives

For decades, the imagination of US pastors and planters has been held captive first by the church growth movement's obsession with numerical growth and then by fearmongering around church decline.

2. New Models

Church planting, like many startup incubators, is constantly engaged in experimentation, trying new forms of missional church and pushing the boundaries of traditional ecclesiologies. Some of these ascendent new models of church include micro-churches, multiethnic churches, and digital churches.

3. Renewed Practices

Ultimately, the work of evangelism happens when we actually "do the work of an evangelist" as Paul exhorts Timothy to do (2 Tim 4:5). This means engaging not necessarily in new practices but in renewing our commitment to historic practices, including prayer, hospitality, and conversation.

Conclusion

Church planting is a means whereby a whole congregation can embody and express the good news of Jesus Christ in highly contextualized ways. For this reason, it will always be a significant and powerful learning lab and testing ground for the church's work of evangelism. May the Spirit empower our work as evangelists through the work of missional leaders and church planters.

Bibliography

Bingham, J. R. "NAMB SBC Report: Ezell Spotlights Disciple-Making Task Force, Church Planting Impact." North American Mission Board, June 14, 2018. https://www.namb.net/news/namb-sbc-report-ezell-spotlights-disciple-making-task-force-church-planting-impact.

Keller, Tim. "Why Plant Churches?" Redeemer City to City, Jan. 1, 2002. https://redeemercitytocity.com/articles-stories/why-plant-churches.

Richardson, J. R. *You Found Me: New Research on How Unchurched Nones, Millennials, and Irreligious Are Surprisingly Open to Christian Faith*. Downers Grove, IL: IVP, 2019.

Tang, Len. "Church Plants as Evangelism Laboratories." *Fuller Magazine* 26 (December 2023) 56–61. https://fullerstudio.fuller.edu/theology/church-plants-as-evangelism-laboratories/.

Wagner, C. P. *Church Planting for a Greater Harvest*. Ventura, CA: Regal, 1990.

Chapter 11

The Incarcerated Church

Reforming the Incarcerated Church

Jarret Keith and Soong-Chan Rah

"You have a prepaid call from an inmate at the California State Prison Los Angeles County. This call and or telephone number will be monitored and recorded."

Student 1: "I was sentenced to forty-two years to life. I've been in for seventeen years and I've been following the Lord since 2017."

Student 2: "The length of my sentence is actually life without the possibility of parole. I've been incarcerated for over thirty years, and I have been honestly and seriously following the Lord for over thirty years."

Student 3: "I've been in prison since February 20, 1998, so it's been Twenty-six years. I was sentenced to life without the possibility of parole, plus twenty years. I will say, you know, the Lord provided me with insight into His love pretty much the whole time. But I think that I actually tapped into His blessings approximately around 2017."

Student 4: "I was sentenced to three consecutive twenty-five-to-life sentences. I've been incarcerated now for twenty-three and a half years. In March of 2023, it will be twenty-four years. I gave my life to Christ on Thanksgiving of 2015 when it actually was the worst day of my life, but it became the best day of my life. I was on the verge of suicide and

Christ came and found me in that prison cell, and I've been walking with the Lord ever since then."

De-Constructing Prison Ministry Evangelism (Voices from the Incarcerated Church)

What have been some helpful and unhelpful aspects of prison ministry efforts?

Student 3: "I know that prison ministry is a spiritual outreach program that is designed to support and provide resources for incarcerated individuals. It's my opinion that this creation by God has been a blessing. It's one of his many ways of displaying His love to me. My favorite book is Romans. Romans 13:10 talks about 'love does no harm.' And I believe that prison ministry is one of God's many ways that has provided love. And I believe that any little thing someone does is a blessing. So I feel fortunate. I look forward to more of God's love flowing through him, whatever prison ministry he sends my way. I appreciate them all."

Student 1: "The helpful part is when we get visitors coming in, it's always great. It's always great when we get to interact with people that are free. Especially for guys that don't get visits or don't have people coming to see them. It's almost like a visit to them. It uplifts people. For a lot of guys that don't have support, it's just knowing that people care about them that are out there. But it goes both ways, because the unhelpful part is that it's rare when you have prison ministries that are long term. Visitors will come in and they may be here a year, two or three years, and then they'll disappear. And then I think, 'What happened to so-and-so, he never came back?' Then we get another prison ministry coming in. After a while, sometimes guys just get a little jaded. You meet people, you build a bond, you build a relationship with a visitor and they don't show up anymore. Then you gotta build another bond with the next visitor."

Student 4: "I would say that people coming from the outside, it's helpful in itself—really just their presence there. Their presence has potential, because the minute someone that's incarcerated sees someone that comes from the outside, it's automatically going to draw them to that person, because it gives them a sense of hope. It shows them that someone cares about them and that they are not forgotten. But to determine if that's going to be helpful or not—it is about the visitor's purpose. What is the purpose of their presence? Is it going to be consistent? Because you have some people that come and then they'll sow a seed and then they'll just disappear. You have to follow up, because a lot of times people get their hopes up. You also have to factor in the trauma that incarcerated people have faced, dealing with abandonment issues and dealing with neglect. A lot of it comes from the church because my father was the preacher, so I grew up in a church, and I hated everything about Christianity because I saw what I perceived to be hypocrites. And so now I'm in prison, and if someone comes from the outside saying, 'Oh, you poor little sinners, I'm just going to preach to you guys.' It becomes condescending. You're re-traumatizing me, because I see my father in you, and not in a good way. So that can be unhelpful."

Student 2: "I've had ministries come in, and one ministry asked me, 'What do you guys need?' And I told him in no uncertain terms, 'We need it all.' Then this ministry went on to express what it is that they could do. 'Do you need praise and worship leaders? Do you need us to come up and hold services? What about a Bible college?' And we replied 'Yes' to all of those things and none of them came through. And so, it reinvigorates the idea that we're insignificant, as if the incarcerated church does not matter at all. When the church makes us feel like that—we're supposed to be taking on a culture of love—and love doesn't ask any questions about your past or about your present condition. Love just says, 'What do you need?' We're experiencing from the outside church, anything but that love. It is a breeding ground for contempt, for destructive thoughts, and it is a breeding ground of a sense of worthlessness. I just can't say enough about it, it's extremely painful. I'm fifty-four years old and I still cry over the treatment that we have experienced from men and women that say that they love us because they love Jesus."

What are some of the challenges the incarcerated church faces to share the gospel inside of the prison, and what are some ways that you have seen the incarcerated church overcome some of those challenges? Also, how can churches and prison ministries come alongside to help the incarcerated church overcome some of those challenges?

Student 1: "So of course, we're incarcerated, so there are the challenges of physical barriers. All the brothers don't live in the same building. We're all scattered around the yard. And you have a lockdown and cancelled services. But that's just part of being in this environment. It comes with it. Also in California, sometimes you have the racial barriers. We're fortunate that the church here does not have to worry about that. In other places or yards, that does become a thing sometimes. But the thing that holds us back is really just physical barriers. It's just the access. For instance, if I'm going through something and I want to reach out to somebody, but they're in another building or they're in a cell down the way. If I were out there, I could just easily call them. But in here, I have to wait until I come out of the cell in order to see them, so I can talk to this person and maybe get some advice."

Student 2: "This Sunday, me and a few gentlemen went to another building with permission—we took a few pastry items and some sodas and we shared the gospel. And it was phenomenal. The crowd that we had and being able to speak to men squarely about the gospel of Jesus Christ was profound. The response was profound. But at the same time, we're limited because we're incarcerated. We're not seen as preachers of the gospel; we're seen as inmates. And because of that, there's security issues. And whenever we go to a building and minister, the staff is not thinking, 'Wow, this is powerful.' No, they're thinking, 'This crowd is getting too big and if something goes wrong it's on them.' If the church outside could network with us, where they could open doors that we can't open—so that the gospel of Jesus Christ can be illuminated throughout this whole institution. How much better would that be?"

Student 3: "The church community that comes into prison isn't actually a part of the community where I come from and the culture where I come from. So, I would like to see more people come from the community that I come from. It's one of my callings to help put a stop to the self-destruction that has plagued some of these inner cities. I believe that if I were able to connect through the church, the Lord will be able to use me to have a positive influence and impact upon the community which I come from. I am doing that either way, but I feel like the church that is already tapped into the community—that will be very powerful for someone like me to be able to communicate with the church. And be able to show them my value and God's love that is blessed upon me and be able to bless the community in which I come from."

Student 4: "What I would like to see from outside churches is their presence. We do feel like we're forgotten about. Where is the church? We have struggles, and we know that the church has the resources to help us in many areas. I would love to see someone from the church come in here and give us some biblical counseling. What does the Bible say about this issue, or if I'm struggling in this area, what is some counseling that I can have that would help me on this path? How about the people that are incarcerated who are married and they're separated from their spouse and they're struggling with that. Or their wife is out there having to raise two or three kids on her own—that's another hurdle. Who do we have to talk to that can give us some advice on how to deal with that situation?"

Student 1: "What we would like to see is prison ministries coming in here to empower the church that is already in here. A lot of prison ministries think that the church is out there. They come in here like we have nothing established and we're just here looking to them for everything. That's not necessarily true. We have a church, a vibrant church, a growing church, and we would like prison ministries to empower our church, to equip our church, to recognize our church and help us in the efforts that we're doing here. The discipleship process, the prison ministries cannot do it, because they are only here on the weekend or once a week. The daily process of discipleship, we're the ones that are building each other up, discipling the new believers. We would like prison ministries to invest in us, to invest in the incarcerated church."

Student 4: " We want to bring hope into people's lives. I can speak for myself and countless other brothers who have given their life to Christ while incarcerated. There was a time when we really didn't have hope and Christ gave us hope. But in order for some people to see that hope, they need to see people in society that actually see our humanity. When I was eighteen, I did some of the most horrible things ever.

But now I'm forty-two years old, and people still see me as that same eighteen-year-old person. The church's absence here is saying that they still see me as that eighteen-year-old person. If I were to get out right now and I went to the church that I went to when I was a child, I'm pretty sure I would be judged."

Student 3: "I'm trying to reach people that come from different places, such as where I come from, that feel like 'I've been through so much. There's no way that God can love me. I've harmed people, I've hurt people.' But I'm here to let them know that Jesus still loves them, and I want people to understand that if he can make a change in a person like me, he can make a change in anybody. I try not to worry about any obstacles, because I always know that there's going to be a door that opens up. I have faith in the Lord, and when we have faith in the Lord, there's nothing that can stop us."

Re-Construction Through an Authentic Incarcerated Church (Jarret Keith)

My own experience with prison ministry reveals that the gospel that was brought in by outsiders was severely limited, communicating messages that had to be unlearned and had actually been harmful. Prison ministry is primarily perceived as an outreach to criminals—to reach people who are fundamentally corrupt, fundamentally evil, fundamentally distorted—and who need help and rescuing. This approach stems from a particular assumption about the message of the gospel: that it primarily exists to reach people who require salvation. Ministries often enter prisons with the belief that the gospel serves as the most effective form of rehabilitation for incarcerated individuals.

Upon reflection, I have found that this entire framework of the gospel has been deeply harmful, both for myself and for others. It further reinforces the message of society that inmates are criminals who are fundamentally evil or corrupt, and maybe society is better off without them, unless they're rehabilitated, or to Christianize it, "transformed." Consequently, the messages delivered focused primarily on God's love and forgiveness, that regardless of any crimes or sins committed, we could be saved and our souls could be set free. The implication was that, through this salvation, individuals could experience joy and peace, even within the confines of prison. Accordingly, all training, equipping, and discipleship provided by these churches and prison ministries centered on how to become a better person and a good citizen.

Looking back, I realized that I wasn't incarcerated because I was more inherently evil than those engaged in prison ministry or anyone else in society. I was incarcerated largely because society failed me from a very young age. My family had failed me from a very young age. I didn't have the solutions or opportunities to thrive in this world that other people had the privilege of accessing. What I, and others who are incarcerated, needed to hear was more about healing the trauma that's been experienced through the journey of being incarcerated. The gospel should address the trauma inflicted by societal oppression and the deep wounds caused by poverty and marginalization.

However, when individuals are viewed primarily as subjects in need of rehabilitation, the true essence of sharing the good news is lost. Thus, the ministries and churches entering the prison system offered no practical solutions for my eventual release, nor for how I would navigate life after incarceration.

It became apparent that I was never considered a potential leader within their community or church. Expectations were set remarkably low with the primary objective that we attend church on Sundays and don't commit any more crimes. Is the community much better for that? I realized that the central message of the gospel, offering abundant life, was largely absent from this version of the good news. I needed to find solutions tailored to the circumstances I faced, the reality of mass incarceration, and the societal barriers encountered by individuals returning from prison. The church and the community, and prison ministries appeared largely unaware or ill-equipped to address these challenges.

Furthermore, when many individuals who were released attempted to reconnect with these ministries, there were multiple barriers to communication and connection. Frequently, they are met with statements such as: "We are not permitted to contact former inmates." "We are not allowed to contact former prisoners." "Exchanging phone numbers is prohibited." "Exchanging emails is not permitted." "Sharing addresses is not allowed." Ultimately, there exists a presumption that formerly incarcerated individuals are fundamentally evil or potentially threatening, even after professing faith in Christ. To perpetuate and reinforce such perceptions is antithetical to the message of the gospel.

Our reality is that individuals from the incarcerated church, whether still inside or recently released, are rarely presented with genuine opportunities to serve and lead. Many are greeted warmly—"Welcome to our church! But come on Sundays and go home like everyone else." There is no acknowledgment of the unique gifts and skills these individuals possess. There is no knowledge of how to practically help somebody who is incarcerated or formerly incarcerated to pursue the call of God on their life. This is not a matter of loving people more. This is not a matter of being nicer or kinder to people. What is required is systemic transformation—a reimagining of what the good news truly means for those who are incarcerated or returning from incarceration.

I know an individual who served within an evangelism association for years as an incarcerated believer. They loved him as a volunteer. He passed out all their materials, helped recruit people, and helped to spread the gospel within the prison system. After more than twenty years of incarceration, he eagerly anticipated the opportunity to serve the Lord upon his release. Having volunteered with this ministry for over five years, he reached out to continue his service with this ministry. However, when he applied to volunteer, he was informed, "You cannot volunteer for our ministry because you do not pass our background check. You have a felony on your record." In my view, such policies are fundamentally contrary to the teachings of Christ and the message of the gospel. Unfortunately, this experience is far from uncommon.

This scenario encapsulates the broader reality of incarceration and evangelism. The issues I have raised—regarding what is the good news communicated to people who are incarcerated and what is the good news for the previously incarcerated when they come home—are vividly illustrated by this individual's experience.

Despite his faithful service for over five years, this believer was rejected by the very ministry he had faithfully served and assisted. Once he was released and sought to serve the Lord and his community, once he no longer had chains on his arms, once he was no longer in a cage, once he was in the community with the desire and a passion to serve the Lord and to serve others as a free man—the ministry slammed the door in his face. I have witnessed this pattern repeatedly—both within churches and parachurch ministries. This is the reality for the incarcerated church.

I believe what is needed now is the establishment of a new table, where incarcerated and formerly incarcerated individuals—the incarcerated church—take the lead in the change that is needed. The incarcerated church can be the change that is needed: to demonstrate the good news, the reality of redemption, and the belief in a gospel that transforms somebody into a new person and a new creation.

Then, when we report that "seventy-five inmates made a confession of faith," or "fifty inmates were baptized in this prison chapel," or "look at these inmates praising the Lord with their hands up in the middle of a prison," but when they come home, they hear, "Oh, we can't actually talk to you." "You can't actually come to my house." "You can't actually serve in our ministry." "You actually are not qualified to be a leader in our church because you have a felony on your record." We must ask ourselves whether this response truly reflects a belief in the good news proclaimed by Jesus—that the gospel has the power to redeem, transform, and restore. Can we genuinely claim to believe this if our actions do not reflect these truths? These experiences are not unique to me, but they are shared by countless other believers in the incarcerated church.

Testimony Ministries serves hundreds of believers who are incarcerated and returning home, and we witness these realities on a daily basis. A central challenge remains the lack of meaningful opportunities. Where are the intentional opportunities for the incarcerated church to be empowered? Where are the intentional opportunities for believers who have been previously incarcerated to be empowered within local churches and ministries?

If intentional opportunities are not being created and made available for this demographic of believers, what does that say about our commitment to spreading the good news? How, then, is the good news truly being demonstrated? We need to be committed to creating such opportunities—to actively demonstrate and embody the good news of Jesus Christ through the testimonies of believers who are currently or formerly incarcerated, the incarcerated church.

A Constructive Theology of the Incarcerated Church (Soong-Chan Rah)

Ministry and evangelism to the incarcerated are shaped by underlying assumptions that warrant critical examination.[1] Questions of who is deemed deserving or worthy of evangelism efforts inevitably invoke power

1. See Alexander, *New Jim Crow*; and Gilliard, *Rethinking Incarceration*.

dynamics, which are often rooted in racial dynamics.[2] The racialized aspects of mass incarceration—and, by extension, ministry to those who are incarcerated—demand critical attention. The disproportionate representation of Black, Brown, and Indigenous individuals within the United States prison system, in particular, necessitates direct confrontation and analysis.[3] Because of the racialized aspect of incarceration, evangelism to—or toward—the incarcerated also becomes racialized.

Willie Jennings argues that "white indicates high salvific probability, rooted in the signs of movement toward God (for example, cleanliness, intelligence, obedience, social hierarchy, and advancement in civilization)."[4] Whites and those who can approximate whiteness and white culture are more likely to respond positively to the gospel. Conversely, other forms of non-whiteness—represented by Black, Brown, and Indigenous bodies—are often met with skepticism regarding their capacity for salvation. Blackness invites a certain amount of doubt and uncertainty regarding their potential saving grace.

Consequently, evangelistic efforts by predominantly white Christian communities toward Black, Brown, or Indigenous communities are often characterized by a perceived need for additional intervention or effort with underlying doubts about the assurance of salvation. With the incarcerated populations in the United States overwhelmingly composed of Black, Brown, and Indigenous individuals, there emerge problematic assumptions: that these bodies are inherently deserving of punishment, more difficult to reach with the gospel, and less capable of developing their own faith. Therefore, the development of evangelistic strategies targeting incarcerated populations may be shaped by racialized assumptions concerning salvific viability.

Evangelism, therefore, is frequently conceptualized through a lens in which the privileged—those presumed to be spiritually and intellectually superior—enter carceral spaces to minister to those deemed morally reprobate, less responsible, less intellectual, and less spiritual. Evangelism to the incarcerated is a truth possessed modality and the transmission of possessed truth to those without the truth. A sense of burden or responsibility among those engaging in prison ministry may emerge, where the privileged perceive themselves as the blessed bearers of religious truth, tasked

2. See Jennings, *Christian Imagination*.

3. See Alexander, *New Jim Crow*; and Davis, *Are Prisons Obsolete?*

4. Jennings, *Christian Imagination*, 35–36.

with transmitting their version of the gospel to a population constructed as less knowledgeable or less blessed.

This framework perpetuates problematic narratives that require critical de-construction, as assumptions about prison evangelism become embedded in a dysfunctional social and theological imagination. An appropriate and thoughtful theological response must be formulated. This response should move beyond sociological assumptions about incarceration and engage a contextually appropriate gospel message.

Walter Brueggemann offers a theological framework that distinguishes between a "theology of celebration" and a "theology of suffering," or, alternatively, a theology of ascent versus descent, and praise versus lament.[5] Those who operate under the theology of celebration, ascent, and praise possess a security and privilege in society. Their worldview is characterized by stewardship and management of their possessions and material blessings. Individuals inhabiting this paradigm often perceive the world as fundamentally good and safe, a reflection of their social location. Life is generally good. Life is generally whole and complete. You are already experiencing shalom because you have a good life in the world that you live in. God, therefore, is a nurturer, a caregiver, a maternal figure who takes care of you. Because life is good and lower tax rates and the power structure benefits you, you seek to maintain the status quo.

Brueggemann posits a theology of suffering as the necessary counter-narrative to celebration. This theology is not marked by management or stewardship, but rather by survival and the need for salvation. The world is not a good place but an evil and challenging place. Life is not healthy and whole, but precarious and always on the edge, marked by hostility, instability and vulnerability. In this context, God is perceived less as a nurturer and more as a warrior, the one who comes to deliver you and smite all your enemies. The status quo, rather than being something to preserve, is understood as a source of harm that must be challenged or transformed. Instead of maintaining the status quo, you fight for justice and resist oppression.[6]

A misapplication of this theological framework may lead to the practice that those situated within the theology of celebration are responsible for imparting their privilege and blessing to those experiencing suffering. The privileged and blessed have nothing to learn or receive from those who are in the context of suffering. However, Brueggemann contends that shalom,

5. See Brueggemann, *Peace*, 26–28.

6. See Brueggemann, *Peace*, 26–28. See also Rah, *Prophetic Lament*, 19–26.

the fullness of God's peace and wholeness, is found in both the theology of celebration and the theology of suffering. An evangelism practice that finds the shalom of God in one space and not the other, yields a dysfunctional theological imagination that requires de-construction.

The gospel of Jesus Christ, therefore, offers the shalom of both suffering and celebration. The gospel is expressed in the crucifixion and death of Jesus on the cross but also in the resurrection of Jesus from the grave. The follower of Jesus may experience pain and suffering in the world, but also embraces the hope of the resurrection and the return of Jesus. The gospel message is incomplete when it is understood unilaterally. Those in celebration and outside of suffering cannot presume they have the complete gospel that they can dump on those without the benefits of privilege and power.

Ministry for and with incarcerated communities thus becomes a unique space where theologies of celebration and suffering are brought into dynamic integration. Believers from both spaces can come together for worship and learning. One side does not have all the answers to simply bestow on the other side, but rather it is a context for mutual engagement and growth. The fullness of the gospel is realized in the coming together of those situated in both celebration and suffering, resurrection and crucifixion. Such integration constitutes an authentic articulation of the gospel message within the context of incarceration.

Bibliography

Alexander, Michelle. *The New Jim Crow: Mass Incarceration in the Age of Colorblindness*. New York: The New Press, 2010.

Brueggemann, Walter. *Peace: Old Testament Understandings and the Christian Church*. St. Louis: Chalice, 2001.

Davis, Angela Y. *Are Prisons Obsolete?* New York: Seven Stories, 2003.

Gilliard, Dominique DuBois. *Rethinking Incarceration: Advocating for Justice That Restores*. Downers Grove, IL: InterVarsity, 2018.

Jennings, Willie James. *The Christian Imagination: Theology and the Origins of Race*. New Haven: Yale University Press, 2010.

Rah, Soong-Chan. *Prophetic Lament: A Call for Justice in Troubled Times*. Downers Grove, IL: InterVarsity, 2015.

List of Contributors

Chapter 1: (Re)forming Evangelism

David Zac Niringiye is an Anglican bishop in the Church of Uganda. His publications include *The Church: God's Pilgrim People* and *The Church in the World: A Historical-Ecclesiological Study of the Church of Uganda with Particular Reference to Post-Independence Uganda, 1962–1992.*

Soong-Chan Rah is the Robert Boyd Munger Professor of Evangelism and Church Renewal at Fuller Theological Seminary, Pasadena, California. His publications include *The Next Evangelicalism: Freeing the Church from Western Cultural Captivity* and *Prophetic Lament: A Call for Justice in Troubled Times.*

Chapter 2: God-Gifted Interruptions

Ruth Padilla DeBorst is the Richard C. Oudersluys Associate Professor of World Christianity at Western Theological Seminary, Holland, Michigan. She also serves with the International Fellowship for Mission as Transformation (INFEMIT), the Community of Interdisciplinary Theological Studies (CETI) and A Rocha Costa Rica.

Chapter 3: Global Evangelism

Vinoth Ramachandra is the former secretary for dialogue and social engagement with the International Fellowship of Evangelical Students. His publications include *Gods That Fail, Subverting Global Myths: Theology and the Public Issues that Shape Our World,* and *Church and Mission in the New Asia.*

Chapter 4: Tom Skinner and Black Power Evangelicalism

Jemar Tisby is research professor of history and African American studies at Fuller Theological Seminary, Pasadena, California. His publications include *The Color of Compromise: The Truth about the Church's Complicity in Racism*, *How to Fight Racism*, and *The Spirit of Justice*.

Chapter 5: Dangerous Women and the Promise of Purity

Jessica Wai-Fong Wong is associate professor of systematic theology at Azusa Pacific University, Azusa, California. Her publications include *Disordered: The Holy Icon and Racial Myths* and *Lamenting Racism: A Christian Response to Racial Injustice* (coauthored).

Chapter 6: Mission as Transformation

Al Tizon is affiliate associate professor of missional and global leadership at North Park Theological Seminary, Chicago, Illinois, and the senior pastor of Grace Fellowship Community Church in San Francisco, California. His publications include *Christ Among the Classes.*

Ruth Padilla DeBorst, Richard C. Oudersluys Associate Professor of World Christianity at Western Theological Seminary, Holland, Michigan.

Chapter 7: Evangelism Among People of Other Faiths

Jose Abraham is associate professor of Islamic studies at Fuller Theological Seminary, Pasadena, California. His publications include *Islamic Reform and Colonial Discourse on Modernity in India: Socio-Political and Religious Thought of Vakkom Moulavi*.

Darren Duerksen is associate professor of intercultural and Christian ministries, program coordinator at Fresno Pacific University, Fresno, California. His publications include *Christ-Followers in Other Religions: The Global Witness of Insider Movements.*

Vinod John is the founding pastor at South Asian Church, Edmonton, Canada. His publications include *Believing Without Belonging? Religious Beliefs and Social Belonging of Hindu Devotees of Christ.*

Chapter 8: Evangelism on Fire

Contributors to this chapter are affiliated with Pentecost Theological Seminary, which was established in 2012 and is located in the Central Region of Ghana in Accra.

David Nyansah Hayfron is area head for The Church of Pentecost in Tarkwa, Ghana and executive council member of The Church of Pentecost.

Amos Jimmy Markin is director of evangelism ministry of The Church of Pentecost, Ghana and executive council member of the Church of Pentecost.

Rebecca Sey is a lifelong missionary who has served in many places with her husband, Aps D. K. Sey (currently the area head for The Church of Pentecost, Dansoman, Ghana).

Christian Tsekpoe is associate professor of Pentecostal–Charismatic Christianity and head of the Center of Ministerial Formation and Training at Pentecost University in Accra, Ghana.

Daniel Okyere Walker is former vice chancellor of Pentecost University and apostle in The Church of Pentecost in Ghana for thirty-one years before retiring in 2021.

Chapter 9: Communal Evangelism from the Margins

Alexia Salvatierra is the academic dean of Centro Latino and associate professor of mission and global transformation at Fuller Theological Seminary, Pasadena, California. She is the author of *God's Resistance: Mobilizing Faith to Defend Immigrants* and coauthor of *Faith-Rooted Organizing: Mobilizing the Church in Service to the World.*

Brandon Wrencher is an organizer, minister, and author. Founder of the Good Neighbor Movement, Greensboro, North Carolina, he is the coauthor of *Buried Seeds: Learning from the Vibrant Resilience of Marginalized Christian Communities.*

Chapter 10: Church Plants as Evangelism Laboratories

Len Tang is the director of the Church Planting Initiative, Fuller Theological Seminary, Pasadena, California. His publications include co-editor and contributor in *Sent to Flourish: A Guide to Planting and Multiplying Churches.*

Chapter 11: The Incarcerated Church

Jarret Keith is the executive director of Testimony Ministries Inc and lead pastor at Church House CA. He oversees Testimony Ministries' work with incarcerated and formerly incarcerated communities, focusing on empowerment and leadership development.

Soong-Chan Rah, Robert Boyd Munger Professor of Evangelism and Church Renewal at Fuller Theological Seminary, Pasadena, California.

Editors

Soong-Chan Rah, Robert Boyd Munger Professor of Evangelism and Church Renewal at Fuller Theological Seminary, Pasadena, California.

Julie B. Scott is a PhD student in the Center for Missiological Research at Fuller Theological Seminary, Pasadena, California. She is coauthor of "Nature of the World," in *The Oxford Handbook for Cognitive Science of Religion* and copy editor for *The Oxford Handbook for Mission Studies.*

Sean M. Watkins is associate dean of Lifelong Learning at Austin Presbyterian Theological Seminary, Austin, Texas, and a PhD student in the Center for Missiological Research at Fuller Theological Seminary, Pasadena, California.

www.ingramcontent.com/pod-product-compliance
Lightning Source LLC
LaVergne TN
LVHW050650100826
845148LV00011B/2058

* 9 7 9 8 3 8 5 2 2 9 9 1 8 *